CHANGE *YOUR* MENOPAUSE!

ABOUT THE AUTHOR

Often referred to as the "godfather of menopause", Wulf Utian, a reproductive endocrinologist and gynecologist, started the world's first center dedicated to menopause research in Cape Town, South Africa, co-founded the International Menopause Society (IMS), and founded both The North American Menopause Society (NAMS) and the Council of Affiliated Menopause Societies (CAMS), all multidisciplinary scientific organizations.

He is Professor Emeritus of Reproductive Biology and Obstetrics and Gynecology at Case Western Reserve University in Cleveland, Ohio. As a practicing physician with over 40 years experience, he worked with thousands of women to help them enhance their quality of life. As an active clinical scientist he has published hundreds of research papers and commentaries. He has been a lecturer and teacher worldwide, and is sought after by the international media, academic centers, and the pharmaceutical industry, for authoritative opinion.

Now he draws on that considerable scientific knowledge and vast clinical experience to provide the real facts about menopause and how it represents the ideal opportunity to take control and enhance the quality of the second half of life.

FIRST REVIEWS

The complete guide to menopause and midlife women's health, written by the world's leading authority and go-to expert on the subject. No one is better qualified than Dr. Wulf Utian, founder of The North American Menopause Society, to demystify menopause, end the confusion about symptoms and treatment options, and provide women with the vital insights and knowledge to take charge of their health and well being. You can finally stop searching - this is the book you've been looking for! **JoAnn E. Manson, MD, DrPH, NCMP, Professor of Medicine and the Michael and Lee Bell Professor of Women's Health, Harvard Medical School, President, The North American Menopause Society, 2011-2012**

No one has explained menopause issues better than Wulf Utian in this book. He clearly shows that individualization is most important in guiding and treating menopause. He successfully carries out his stated goal "making recommendations for medical practice based on the interpretation at any one time of the entire body of evidence currently available." This enables the reader to understand choices available to her. I would recommend this book to all women before, during, and after menopause, and to all of those who are involved in their care. **Lila Nachtigall, MD, Professor of Gynecology, New York University**

I doubt you could find a better book by a better and more informed author than Wulf Utian's □*"Change Your Menopause."* If you are one of the millions of women (and some men) confused and anxious about menopause and the big question, whether to take hormones or not, this readable and informative book will help clarify the research and guide you in your decision making. **Phyllis Greenberger, MSW, President & CEO, Society for Women's Health Research**

In this book Dr. Utian combines his experience as a scientist and an educator with what he has learned from years of listening to women in clinical practice and presents what is known about menopause. He focuses on how each woman navigating this pivotal time in her life can take care of herself - an effort that requires individualization - a concept lacking in much written on this important, complex subject. **Marcie Richardson, MD, Director, Harvard Vanguard Menopause Consultation Service**

Dr. Wulf Utian, world-renowned gynecologist and founder of The North American Menopause Society, shares his vast expertise in a warm and friendly style. Readers will appreciate his candor and sound advice. **Margery Gass, MD, NCMP, Executive Director, The North American Menopause Society**

Change Your Menopause is a book written by one of the most authoritative authors in the field, who created the first menopause clinic in the world, founded both the North American Menopause Society and the International Menopause Society to help scientists and health professionals study the most updated scientific information in the field and help women to understand it. This book should become the best reference for a woman to get the right answers to her questions. **Regine Sitruk-Ware, MD, Reproductive Endocrinologist, Distinguished Scientist of the Population Council, New York.**

Dr. Utian and this terrific book embody the "Speaking of Women's Health" mantra of "Be Strong, Be Healthy, and Be in Charge." Dr. Utian, an internationally acclaimed women's health and menopause expert, gives you the information, tools, and choices to individually navigate through midlife and emerge stronger and wiser. **Holly L. Thacker, MD, FACP, CCD, NCMP, Director, Center for Specialized Women's Health, The Cleveland Clinic, and Executive Director, Speaking of Women's Health**

As Executive Producer of the movie *Hot Flash Havoc*, I meet thousands of women challenged by their age, their changing lives, their changing health, and how they want to face their "Second Act." Having great advice to face yourself and others head on and to realize there are no problems, only solutions, can change your life in a positive manner. Wulf Utian is a master in making you think and meet these challenges from an informed decision. **Heidi Houston, Executive Producer, *Hot Flash Havoc*, a movie of menopausal proportions**

Dr. Utian's 40+ years of research and clinical practice in women's health combined with his humor and communication skills have created a "must-read" book for women as they journey through menopause and life after. The book provides accurate, easy-to-read common sense information women need to be informed decision makers regarding their health through mid-life and beyond. **Marilyn Rothert, PhD, FAAN, RN, Dean and Professor Emerita, Michigan State University, College of Nursing**

Confused about menopause? Confused about who is an expert about menopause? You have found the right book. Dr. Wulf Utian is an internationally recognized expert. He tells it like it is. While the truth about menopause and hormones (or not) seems to change on a daily basis, Dr. Utian knows the facts. This easy-to-follow book will help any one searching for reliable, medically sound information about what menopause is; why every woman's experience with menopause is unique; and smart choices to make to ease into this next phase of life. **Susan Wysocki, WHNP, FAAN, President & CEO, National Association of Nurse Practitioners in Women's Health**

Once more we are fortunate to have an updated version of the outstanding 1980 book by Dr. Wulf Utian, *Your Middle Years: A Doctors Guide For Today's Woman*. His work revolutionized our understanding of the menopause and provided a readable guidebook to managing the sometimes-difficult transition of what he termed "women's middle years." As the Founder of the University of California San Diego School of Medicine's Menopause Education Clinic, I recommend this highly readable and useful up-to-date book with enthusiasm.
Sonia Hamburger, Clinical Instructor (retired), Reproductive Medicine Department, University of California San Diego, School of Medicine

Do not underestimate the title of this book, *Change Your Menopause; A Doctor Explains Why One Size Does Not Fit All*. Very few physicians have the skill or the interest in educating and empowering their patients by giving them knowledge about their bodies. How amazing and lucky for his patients and now his readers that Dr. Utian has been the leading researcher and clinician in menopause for decades. In this user-friendly book, Dr. Utian effectively synthesizes a vast amount of information about the complexities of menopause. For menopausal women and the partners who love them, a book like this has been long overdue. **Sheryl Kingsberg, PhD, Professor of Reproductive Biology and Psychiatry, Case Western Reserve University**

Professor Wulf Utian is one of the world's top experts on women's health. In this new book on menopause, he gives women both answers and action points that are essential for women to maximize their health and quality of life. It's about putting the woman at the center and giving her control and the options to cope with menopause and beyond. An excellent approach - I will recommend it to my patients. **Bev Lawton, ONZM, MB.CHB, Dip Obst, FRNZGP, Director, Women's**

Health Research Centre, University of Otago New Zealand. Past President, Australasian Menopause Society

Today there is a realistic expectation that women will live for decades after the menopause. This book informs and guides choices which women may make about their lifestyle and healthcare. It is written in an accessible manner by one of the leading authorities in the care of the older woman. Professor Wulf Utian has dedicated his professional life to postmenopausal health and this is a valuable addition to the literature available for women who wish to be informed about opinions and choices in healthcare. **Zephne M van der Spuy, MD, PhD, FRCOG Professor in Obstetrics and Gynaecology, University of Cape Town, South Africa**

CHANGE _YOUR_ MENOPAUSE!

Why One Size Does Not Fit All

OTHER BOOKS BY WULF UTIAN

The Menopause Manual – A Woman's Guide to the Menopause (MTP Press, Lancaster, UK, 1978)

Menopause in Modern Perspective (Appleton-Century-Crofts, 1980)

Your Middle Years: A Doctor's Guide for Today's Woman (Appleton-Century-Crofts, 1980)

The Premenstrual Syndrome, Pieter van Keep, Wulf H. Utian (MTP Press, Lancaster, UK, 1981)

The Controversial Climacteric, Pieter van Keep, Wulf H. Utian, Alex Vermuelen (MTP Press, Lancaster, UK, 1982)

Multidisciplinary Perspectives on Menopause, Marcha Flint, Fredi Kronenberg, Wulf Utian (*Annals of the New York Academy of Sciences,* Volume 592, June 13, 1990)

Managing Your Menopause, Wulf H. Utian, Ruth S. Jacobowitz (Prentice Hall Press, New York, NY,1990)

The Menopause and Hormonal Replacement Therapy: Facts and Controversies, Regine Sitruk-Ware, Wulf H. Utian (Marcel Dekker, New York, NY, 1991)

THE UTIAN STRATEGY: is this my problem or is this your problem? (Utian Press, Beachwood, Ohio, 2010)

CHANGE _YOUR_ MENOPAUSE!

Why One Size Does Not Fit All

A doctor's authoritative guide to menopause, healthy aging, and the path to enhanced quality of life for today's women

Wulf H. Utian

MD, PhD. DSc (Med), FRCOG, FACOG, FICS

UTIAN PRESS
Beachwood, Ohio

Copyright © 2011 by Wulf H. Utian

UTIAN PRESS
Beachwood, Ohio
www.utianllc.com

First Edition, September 2011

ISBN 978-0-9828457-2-1 (print edition)

ISBN 978-0-9828457-3-8 (eBook edition)

Library of Congress Control Number: 2011912088
Library of Congress Subject Headings:
1. Menopause – Popular works.
2. Menopause-Hormone therapy-Popular works
3. Middle-aged women- Health and hygiene-Popular works

Cover design: Red Flag, Johannesburg, South Africa

To my patients
and
research volunteers

ACKNOWLEDGEMENTS

Over 40 years of experience as a practicing gynecologist and reproductive endocrinologist, teacher, administrator, and researcher, does not occur in a vacuum. There is an endless list of people all over the world to whom I owe an enormous debt of gratitude. This book is the summation of that experience and my tribute to them all.

For the development of this book itself, firstly I thank Sonia Hamburger of San Diego and formerly UC San Diego for constantly cajoling me "Wulf you have to do a follow up to *Your Middle Years*!" I thank my wife Moira for living through yet another project with a deadline (however much it kept moving), and together with my dear friend Nina Kovensky for reading every section, and giving me the feedback I needed whether I liked it or not. I appreciate advice from Peta Moskowitz and Jan Ginsburg. I am humbled by the time Vivian Pinn, MD, Director of the Office of Women's Health Research for 20 years, gave to writing the Foreword in the same month she was planning her retirement. I thank Kathy Wisch, Medical Editor at NAMS, for her supreme editing skills and the time after work that she committed. I am also deeply indebted to Marcie Richardson, MD, Director of the Harvard Vanguard Menopause Consultation Service, for her unflinching and critical medical expert review of the manuscript. Thank you also to my close colleagues who agreed to read the draft and write the early reviews.

I make extensive use of material from scientific position statements, textbooks, and research papers that I have been involved with over the years. In particular, I acknowledge use of the Hormone Therapy Position Statements of The North American Menopause Society (NAMS) and the NAMS Isoflavone Report, of which I have been Panel Chairman throughout, which were published in the NAMS scientific journal, *MENOPAUSE*. I acknowledge the major effort my colleagues have put into helping develop these important documents. I also acknowledge utilizing materials from the National Institutes of Health National Center for Complementary and Alternative Medicine website for coverage on the alternative therapies, particularly because this is the definitive scientific forum to differentiate the effective from the harmful.

I thank my daughter Lara Utian Preston and her company Red Flag in Johannesburg, South Africa, for the cover design. I also thank Curtis McEwen for being so readily available with his remarkable computer skills every time I needed urgent assistance.

Above all, I thank my patients and the women who volunteered over the years for my research projects. I learned a lot from them, and have tried to incorporate all those pearls of wisdom into this manuscript.

Contents

FOREWORD

Dr. Wulf H. Utian undertakes an important and daunting challenge in *Change Your Menopause:* to present and explain, in clear, readily understood language, what is known scientifically about menopause. This book prepares the reader to reflect on her own menopausal circumstances and experiences so that she may have an informed discussion with her clinician and make knowledgeable decisions regarding her own health and quality of life.

A major aspect of Dr. Utian's challenge is to dispel the confusion caused by contradictory and sometimes invalid information about menopause and treatment of its undesired symptoms. In doing so, he presents reliable scientific findings that result from validly designed research studies. A multitude of conceptual and logistic requirements underlie research studies which are intended to determine the causes, effects, and control of a disease, condition, or normal body changes, especially those that may affect every woman. Dr. Utian explains what elements a study must have in order to produce reliable results. He also provides a critique of reports that may be questionable.

Providing trustworthy information is the book's first critical step in helping women chart the course of their health maintenance. The next step is providing an approach to personalizing that information. No two women or their bodies are exactly alike and the combined personal, social, and life circumstances as well as the lifestyle and behaviors of each individual are different mosaic, indeed, a kaleidoscope, of elements to consider in making personal health decisions. Many individuals do not have the full knowledge or information needed to understand the complex elements of a valid research study and, most important, whether the results apply to themselves.

As Director of the Office of Research on Women's Health (ORWH), I can appreciate Dr. Utian's book in the national context of women's health research. It is only in the last 20 years that the National Institutes of Health (NIH) has implemented a policy requiring that women be included routinely in medical and behavioral research as well as to implement many efforts to increase what we know about women's health in general. In 1990, the ORWH was established at NIH to ensure the inclusion of women in clinical research, as well as to expand and enhance research in order to address gaps in knowledge about both women's normal processes and aging, and the diseases or conditions that may affect them.

One major focus during those 20 plus years has been to promote research on women's health during the menopausal transition and the postmenopausal years. Research has been conducted to clarify the menopausal process and to explore environmental, cultural, and lifestyle influences on menopause, and the effects of hormones, including menopausal hormone therapy, on the body.
Although this body of studies has yielded some important results, 20 years is a very short time in the research continuum, especially for a condition as complex as the

menopausal transition and its possible long-term effects on a woman's life. (National Library of Medicine has partnered with ORWH to create the Women's Health Resources Web portal: www.womenshealthresources.nlm.nih.gov. This site gives researchers and consumers access to the latest information about significant topics in women's health from scientific journals, peer-reviewed sources, NIH Institutes and Centers, and health news sources).

To continue making significant progress in the scientific knowledge about menopause, in 2009-2010 ORWH reviewed the national state-of-the-art of women's health research and conducted a process to set NIH priorities for women's health and sex differences research for the next 10 years. The resulting report, *Moving into the Future with New Dimensions and Strategies: a Vision for 2020 for Women's Health Research* (ORWH, NIH, DHHS, Publication Number 10-7606), includes the following goal:

> *Goal #3: Actualize personalized prevention, diagnostics, and therapeutics for women and girls.*

Personalized medicine considers individual differences in genetics, biology, and health history. A comprehensive approach to personalized medicine must take into account biological sex and age as well as health disparities stemming from such factors as social and cultural influences.

A woman's health can be influenced by her behavioral characteristics interacting with genetic and biological factors. In fact, her individual experience of health and disease involves her attitudes, beliefs, emotions, and lifestyle choices and actions—all influenced, in turn, by her race, ethnicity, age, education, employment status, income level, social roles and support system, and sexual preference, among other contributing factors. Her health is also affected by where she lives, her access to quality healthcare, and whether or not she is the victim of violence or physical/sexual abuse. The combination of these factors, and their interaction with her genetic makeup and current physical condition, contribute to a woman's overall health and her susceptibility to disease. They also contribute to what her experience will be of the menopausal transition to the postmenopausal years.

In *Change Your Menopause!* Dr. Utian suggests an approach for women to take action and personalize their menopausal health. He calls this action plan the "Get Up and Go Lifestyle." It consists of four components:

1. Self-education on the facts about midlife and health
2. Twelve basic principles
3. Eight essential tools
4. Eight critical actions

The reader therefore will find this book to be a valuable resource of readily understood information summarizing what has been learned from research studies, as well as a guide to taking responsibility and control, in consultation with her clinician about her own menopausal health.

Dr. Utian is well qualified to take on this challenge. He is considered one of the most significant authorities today on menopause and women's health issues, and he is a dedicated advocate for women's health. He is the Executive Director Emeritus and Honorary Founding President of the North American Menopause Society (NAMS) and is one of the three founders in 1976 of the International Menopause Society. He serves on a number of national and international committees, and has received numerous national and international honors and awards. His expertise on menopause has been recognized through his many invited scientific lectures and media appearances. Dr. Utian has written over 200 papers related to women's health, and has authored five books on menopause. He is the founding editor of *Menopause*, NAMS' official scientific journal.

As women's health research has advanced and expanded, so have studies of the normal processes involved in the menopausal transition and related events in a woman's life course. However, not all studies give clear results, and there are still areas that we need to clarify so that individual women will have the best guidance for making decisions about their menopausal state. Meanwhile, women need a tool for understanding the current scientific implications that will help them formulate, in consultation with their physicians, their personal approach to this important time in their lives. Dr. Utian's book is that valuable tool.

Vivian W. Pinn, MD
Office of Research on Women's Health
National Institutes of Health
Department of Health and Human Services
Bethesda, Maryland

INTRODUCTION

"No self-respecting American woman would read a book with the word "*MENOPAUSE*" on the cover!"

The year was 1979, the city New York, and the speaker, a senior vice president of Appleton, the publishing company, was a woman in a room full of women except me as the lone male. My first book for women had been published the previous year in the United Kingdom under the title *The Menopause Manual*, and Appleton had negotiated the United States rights, provided that I would 'Americanize' the book. So it was published under the title: *Your Middle Years: a doctor's guide for today's woman.*

Fast forward to 2011 and the word *Menopause* is pervasive – used freely in open discussion, the media, musicals, movies, major marketing of all sorts of purported remedies and scams, websites, tweets, Facebook entries, and on and on – and yet despite all that it is still largely misunderstood. Moreover, the medical therapies to relieve symptoms remain a source of major confusion, not only amongst women but also with so many of the physicians, nurse clinicians, and other health providers serving this population.

I am often asked what a man can possibly know about menopause. That is a very fair question. Most men know little and are not too empathetic about "the whole thing." My interest started at age 25 when as a young physician seeking an academic career in gynecology I was intrigued by the iniquitous practice of removing ovaries from reproductive aged women at the time of hysterectomy. Those were the days when women stayed in hospital for a week or more after surgery and I was concerned by the unexplained rapid onset of hot flashes that they developed. I completed a PhD on the physical and biological effects of that procedure, (The clinical and metabolic effects of oophorectomy and the role of replacement of exogenous estrogen therapy, University of Cape Town, 1970), and over the next 40 plus years experienced the menopause transition, the positive and the negative, with literally thousands of women. That experience, combined with my research, teaching, and public speaking with women's groups, must count in favor of a "man in menopause."

A friend of mine complained recently that television, the press, and magazines were full of articles or comments about estrogens and menopause, but that the more she read the less she knew or understood. This seemed most unfortunate, as the subject is one of such direct importance to every woman.

Many good books exist explaining the history and reasons for either the overselling of medications or the under-provision of health care to women traversing the menopause and beyond. Another recapitulation of this old history is not necessary, and is not an objective of mine. Nonetheless, when explaining an issue, if a scientific study has flaws, I will not hesitate to bring the necessary facts to your attention.

Accordingly, this book is a menopause manual. As a story and reference book, it is meant to be read initially like a novel, and then kept for constant reference when the need arises. Only remember this storybook has a difference. It is true to life, and the main character is you, the reader. Moreover, the stakes are high – potentially a healthy and effective life on the one hand, or possible ignorance, missed opportunities, impaired health, and discontent on the other.

This book is a concise explanation of the current facts based on the latest research, and written by an author with the credentials and authority to do so (see "Author's Biographical Sketch," Appendix D). The challenge has been to provide a straightforward explanatory book that is scientifically accurate yet easy to read and understand. I therefore stand responsible for the decision to present the facts in clear-cut language uncluttered by references. However, all statements are scientifically substantiated.

Within these pages, you will find all the facts about menopause. Ideas and recommendations for a different and exciting lifestyle after menopause will be presented. Hopefully, you will take the facts to heart and heed the advice.

Instead of utilizing or referring to the term "health provider" (a term I hate because of the impersonal relationship it connotes), and in the absence of a good collective term for the doctor, nurse clinician, or other trained professionals you will need to work with, I will use the term Clinician to apply to any or all of these professionals. For the purpose of editorial consistency and simplicity, the pronoun "she" will be used when referring to the "clinician."

Three other important reader advisories:

- Technical and medical terms are marked in *italics* when mentioned for the first time. Generally, they will also be explained at that point. However, you can always refer to the glossary at the end of the book if you need clarification of a medical word or abbreviation.
- Sometimes for those readers who want more detail, I may present more information than most want or feel they need to know. I will present that extra detail in a smaller print size.
- Perimenopause means "around menopause," and so is not separated from "menopause' in this book.

Although this book is intended as a complete guide to menopause, it is not a pharmaceutical do-it-yourself kit. In other words, where medications and medical care are necessary, don't try any shortcuts. See your clinician. The big difference is that when you do so, you will be well informed, and able to discuss things on a one-to-one basis.

In the long run, each of us must take responsibility for the quality of our own lives and the health care we receive. Whether you are a woman already approaching midlife or beyond menopause, the purpose of this book is to give you insight into menopause and older women's health, and the potential therapies, including hormones. Then you can meaningfully discuss your own health requirements on a level basis with your clinician at an appropriate time. I will also discuss potential therapies for those who need them, including hormones. If this book helps in this vital area of decision making, leading to enhanced quality of life, it will have amply achieved its purpose.

CHAPTER 1

OUR BODIES ARE DIFFERENT

Surely women are women? Of course women have specific similarities, but it is their differences that serve to drive home the subtitle of this book, namely, in contemporary menopause management, *one size does not fit all*! I will return to this subject shortly, but first it is necessary to provide the background information to menopause and its appropriate management.

Let me emphasize one point immediately. Until the late 1990's, whenever the word menopause came up in some medical circles, it was almost universally equated with another term "*Hormone Replacement Therapy* (HRT), as if the one could not get along without the other. This implied you could not be fully active or healthy after menopause unless you took hormonal medication. Today, a new philosophy prevails.

Contemporary menopause management is a complex subject involving many aspects of preventing or treating both minor and major medical problems, requiring on occasion advanced diagnostic technologies, and incorporating a broad range of potential treatments, starting with the most noninvasive such as changes in lifestyle, and progressing to some new and very complicated pharmaceutical products.

WHAT IS MENOPAUSE?

Here is the official definition (NAMS, 2010): The word *menopause* implies permanent cessation of ovulation and menses. *Spontaneous* or *natural* menopause is said to have occurred after 12 months without a period (*amenorrhea)* with no pathologic cause. It reflects a near-complete but natural diminution of ovarian hormone secretion. There is no adequate biological marker for menopause.

In simple English, *menopause* means the last, final, and never-to-return loss of the monthly menstrual period, a natural event through which all women will eventually traverse.

But if only it was that simple. To many women worldwide it is as much a state of mind as it is a state of bodily change. There are numerous descriptions, misconceptions, and even marketed untruths (yes, lying for purpose of gain) as to what the "change of life" is really all about. Few of these stories match each other, except that none ever paint a pretty picture of what to expect.

To most people, even the clinicians, menopause means more in their minds than the final menstrual period. Rather, it is a word used to collectively include the final period, as well as years before and many years after, and a host of real or perceived symptoms and potential diseases. I will not try and struggle against the headwinds, but instead will broaden my use of the word so that we can just get on with business and deal with the essential issues. Europeans tend to use *climacteric* (Greek: steps of a ladder) instead of menopause to refer to this time in a woman's life.

Given the great mythology that has built up around the word menopause it is little wonder that many women approach this significant event with nothing short of dread, anxiety, and fear. In desperation, most women turn for guidance to friends or family, to women's magazines, to the Internet, or the lay medical press (confirmed information through Gallup polls). What do they get out of this? Mostly confused – a confusion that may aggravate an already existing distorted image of life and where it is going.

- "There is nothing to it," says one friend, but "it is the change of life and beginning of old age," says another.
- "My sex life ended and my husband left me," confides her next-door neighbor, while her aunt warns: "Take life easy or you will break a bone!"
- "Menopause is a galloping catastrophe," stated one early renowned physician who hurried to add that with hormone therapy, "you will be much more pleasant to live with and will not become dull and unattractive."
- "You must really be crazy to allow a male chauvinist gynecologist prescribe you hormones. Don't you know they cause cancer and heart attacks?" shouts her daughter.

And so it goes on and on, with increasing confusion, more indecision, hot flashes, night sweats, and greater emotional distress, the escalating and inevitable results.

Whose fault is this distorted idea of menopause? Probably ignorance aided and abetted by social attitudes, fallacies, and misconceptions. The situation, moreover, has often been traded upon by groups as disparate as the fashion industry, parts of the medical profession including most notably the cosmetic surgeons, the pharmaceutical industry, sports good producers, snake oil salesman, the compounding pharmacy and *bioidentical hormone* movement, and operators of spa and health farms. This list is not complete!

Yet this common distorted image of menopause is not pervasive throughout our society, and certainly not in many parts of the world. Do you know that:

- Some women really do look forward to menopause?
- The average European woman has less anxiety about menopause and aging than her American sister?
- In Japan there is not even a word in the language to describe a hot flash?
- Stresses and strains are placed on many people, not just aging women, by the so-called "youth culture"?
- A change in your sex life is not inevitable?
- If you are considering taking hormones but are not certain what to do, there is a whole new body of evidence as well as carefully considered medical recommendations from leading scientific organizations that can assist you in your decision?
- Before making decisions about your menopausal potential treatments, you really need to know the facts about them?

I will try in these pages to provide answers to these questions and many more. Written expressly for the concerned woman, it would be a wise idea for men to read it too. They need a lot of insight into menopause, as well as some understanding of the women with whom they associate. Men should know that male menopause is in some ways as real an entity as the female counterpart, and many principles and lessons presented in this book could well apply to them.

My intention is to make facts understandable. Although I write in consumer language the facts are scientific. If you feel inspired to read in greater depth, the suggested list of references and information sources at the end of the book will show you the way.

Medical research is accelerating at a furious pace. Any medically oriented book could be criticized for being out of date even before it is published. Such criticism is only true about the leading edge of research. An understanding of the basic facts is necessary before new aspects of research can be appreciated. This book should provide you with these basic building blocks. Thereafter, you can more appropriately evaluate and recognize whether each new piece of information is a genuinely real advance.

Let me quote from a statement that appears repeatedly in the position statements for various menopausal treatments presented by the Scientific Panels of *The North American Menopause Society (NAMS):*

Evidence-based medicine implies that recommendations be limited to the women for whom the studies are relevant. Although this goal is ideal in principle, it is impossible in practice, given that there will never be adequate randomized, controlled trials covering all populations, eventualities, drugs, and drug regimens. The practice of medicine is ultimately based on the interpretation at any one time of the entire body of evidence currently available. The Panel accepted the fact that no trial data can be used to extrapolate clinical management recommendations for the entire female population and that no single trial should be used to make public health recommendations.

That is what I will be doing in these pages – coming to conclusions and making recommendations for medical practice "based on the interpretation at any one time of the entire body of evidence currently available."

Menopause is much more than hormones. Other aspects, such as the way you live your life, sexual activity, and the attitudes of society, will also be considered. The positive concept that I will present to you as a new lifestyle after menopause is based on straightforward principles that really work.

Very little in life that is genuinely worthwhile comes easily. This book is no more than a guide or practical handbook, much the equivalent of a computer or new car instruction manual that needs to be understood. The difference is that the appliance described is *you*. After reading it, you will be better able to judge your own needs after menopause, hormonal and other, and "change of life" can truly be made to mean, "change for the better."

CHAPTER 2

MENOPAUSE - WHAT'S THE BIG DEAL?

Menopause is important at three levels:

1. As a lead indicator of changing demographics: a signal event highlighting the gradual demise of the dominating youth culture and the growing impact of aging populations
2. As a driver of public health policy: a marker in the life cycle of women that identifies and determines the potential for risk factor identification, early disease diagnosis, leading to reduction of disability and its attendant health care costs
3. The personal level: enhancing quality of life through appropriate changes in personal behavior and appropriate medical management

I will only give a brief overview of the first two of these issues because of their critical importance in relation to health policy, the economy, their political challenge, and the potential demand for expensive delivery of medical services. The remainder of the book will address item 3.

1. CHANGING POPULATION DEMOGRAPHICS AND VITAL STATISTICS

No woman needs fear that she stands alone as she approaches menopause. There has been a real increase in the actual number of women reaching and living well beyond this time. The median age at natural menopause is 51.3 years (that is, the age at which 50% of American women will have transitioned though menopause). Media headlines have warned: NEW POPULATION TRENDS TRANSFORMING United States. These trends really do exist. They are occurring throughout the world and have far-reaching implications for the future.

Some countries have high birth rates resulting in more young people. These are usually developing nations where disease rates are higher resulting in greater infant mortality. Even these countries are showing major growth in the population of older people. An example of a high birth rate country would be Mexico.

Other countries have low growth rates. Fewer babies and better health services result in more people living to an older age. These are invariably the more developed countries. Japan and Sweden are good examples. Russia too has a greater population of older individuals but is less developed than Japan or Sweden.

The United States falls somewhere between Mexico and Sweden. The population statistics are quite striking. In 1900, the median age of people in the United States was 22.9 years. By 1950, it was 30.2. It was around 35 at the turn of the century and is projected to be 37.3 by the year 2030. This means the average age of the population is gradually increasing. The increased number of people living to an old age can be more easily imagined if you realize that 1 in 10 of the population today is over age 65. By 2030, this figure may be 1 in 6.

There is unequivocal evidence that the population of women over age 50 has changed significantly over the course of history. The life expectancy for a woman born during the time of the Roman Empire was about 29 years. During the late medieval period, this increased to 33 years. By 1841, in England and Wales, the average female life expectancy had reached 42 years. A dramatic change developed during the late nineteenth and early twentieth centuries; the expectation of life at birth had increased to 74.9 years by 1970, and closer to 80 by 2011. So in just the past century, life expectancy has almost doubled.

Of course, all those years ago there were women who lived to a very ripe old age. Looking at how many years a woman was likely to live from birth onward can be very misleading. Most women historically died from complications of childbirth or the effects of various epidemics, and fewer were left to live into old age. Another way of looking at the numbers is to consider how long a woman can be expected to live if she is healthy at age 50. This has increased from about 20.6 years in 1900 to about 30 years in 2000. Only now more women have been reaching the increased age, and for each decade over age 50 that they remain well, the final number gets larger. It is thus possible that the modern woman can anticipate spending virtually half of her life after menopause!

There are no exact figures for the absolute number of postmenopausal women, or the number reaching menopause on an annual basis. In the Unites States, there were an estimated 45.6 million postmenopausal women in 2000. This number is expected to increase to more than 50 million older than age 51 by 2020. In Canada, it is estimated that by 2026 almost a quarter (22%) of the Canadian population will be composed of women older than 50. Worldwide, the number of postmenopausal women is expected to rise to 1.1 billion by 2025.

Life expectancy for men has not matched that for women. This creates an increasing proportion of single or widowed women. Unless the death rate for men is drastically cut, the gap in life-span between men and women is likely to widen, even though both live longer.

The bottom line is that more women are living longer, and consequently have more time to be exposed to illnesses, some of which are related to or impacted by menopause. But the number of older men also continues to increase, driving the average age of the population ever higher, and the likelihood of more of these individuals requiring expensive long-term health care becomes ever greater.

2. PUBLIC HEALTH POLICY AND HEALTHCARE IMPLICATIONS

Consider what all the above means in terms of changes in housing requirements, land use, medical care, recreational facilities, rehabilitation centers, retirement, health insurance and costs, senior centers, long-term care facilities, and so forth. On the flip side, school enrollments drop, a smaller younger population carries an ever-increasing financial burden, and the generation gap becomes a potential burden on all.

No wonder politicians on both sides of the U. S. Congress are arguing about Medicare, Social Security, and health insurance. Not to worry, I do not intend to get into politics at all. But I do have to be a realist, and state categorically that we face a tide of misery unless radical actions are taken in regard to healthcare.

Menopause as a marker in the female life cycle offers one opportunity that public policy experts and politicians should grab – to reduce long-term health costs by enhancing health-related quality of life. But it highlights a very significant *Catch-22*.

Pardon me if I take a detour and address the problem of a *Catch-22*. Remember Joseph Heller's 1961 novel, *Catch-22*?

There was only one catch and that was Catch-22, which specified that a concern for one's safety in the face of dangers that were real and immediate was the process of a rational mind. Orr was crazy and could be grounded. All he had to do was ask; and as soon as he did, he would no longer be crazy and would have to fly more missions. Orr would be crazy to fly more missions and sane if he didn't, but if he was sane he had to fly them. If he flew them he was crazy and didn't have to; but if he didn't want to he was sane and had to. Yossarian was moved very deeply by the absolute simplicity of this clause of Catch-22 and let out a respectful whistle. "That's some catch, that Catch-22," he observed. "It's the best there is," Doc Daneeka agreed.

Well the catch-22 in our fractured US health system is called *preventive care*. In truth, there is little we can do to truly prevent (if that really means stopping the likelihood of it ever occurring), apart from some of the remarkable vaccines against infections. What we can do for many of the most prevalent of the diseases of older age is *reduce the likelihood* of getting them, or at least *reduce the severity and the complications.* But that is not the catch-22.

No, this is a much more serious issue. Let me give a very personal experience that explains the dilemma quite dramatically. I was invited some years back to give a lecture in Los Angeles at a dinner meeting that was preceding a major conference for executives of health insurance companies, management care organizations, healthcare facilities, private hospital groups, the pharmaceutical industry, and others. I was seated at dinner with the CEO of one of the nation's largest providers of health insurance (who shall remain nameless, because his response reflects the nature of the beast we are facing). After the main course, I was invited to speak, which I did on my favorite topic of using menopause as a marker to bring women back into the health care system; most withdraw after they have completed childbearing and do not return unless ill. The purpose from a public health policy perspective is to utilize the menopause as an entry point into a comprehensive screening program to identify risk for future disease or early stages of existing disease. The sooner preventive measures or early treatments are introduced, the greater the likelihood of reducing the serious outcomes, which also happen to be the most expensive procedures for those diseases. In other words, an ounce of prevention could save a pound of treatment.

Quite pleased with myself that I had given one of my better performances, I sat down again at my table. The CEO addressed me immediately. "You know, Wulf, I completely agree with you about the need for population screening and early introduction of appropriate measures. But of course you must realize that all the bad diseases that you are aiming at, like broken hips, heart attacks, Alzheimer's disease and so on, only truly present themselves in older populations, that is over age 65. That is Medicare. That is the government's dime. Why should my company spend money up front on prevention when the government will pay for treating the diseases later? It is just not sound business!"

I was floored, and put off eating my dessert. The fact is that barely 1% of our entire healthcare expenditure goes out on preventive care, and that is the truth.

Not surprising then that our health system is so well organized for what I call "crisis care." Suffer a heart attack on Main Street and an emergency team will be there in minutes, usually getting you rapidly to an Intensive Care Unit, where the best modern care will be available. Hopefully, of course, you have health insurance. But if your clinician prescribes a medication for preventive healthcare, then almost certainly your health insurance will deny payment.

So here is the catch-22 of appropriate menopause management. Menopause is the perfect opportunity to check for risk factors and undiagnosed disease. But the medical insurance industry has little incentive to spend money in the present for complications of diseases that will mostly express themselves after age 65, which is when Medicare covers them. So if you get the tests before 65, the insurance company usually will not pay. If you don't get an early diagnosis for risk of a disease, or an early stage of established disease, the complications and outcome will be worse later. And the treatment will usually be more expensive. The catch-22 is a sick healthcare industry.

Perhaps it is time for the veritable army of menopausal women I described above to get militant and demand of their politicians and policy makers that our healthcare system be brought into the modern age for everyone!

CHAPTER 3

SOME NECESSARY BASIC SCIENCE

In order to understand the true effects of menopause, the potential real symptoms, and the possible diseases that may be related, it is necessary to explain a little *anatomy, physiology, molecular biology,* and *pathology*. Where I get carried away with presenting a little more detail than may be necessary, feel free to gloss over the small print.

ANATOMY: The science of the structure of the human body
PHYSIOLOGY: The science relating to the functions of the living organism and its parts
MOLECULAR BIOLOGY: The study of molecular structures and events underlying biological processes, including the relation between genes and the functional characteristics they determine
PATHOLOGY: The branch of medicine that treats the essential nature of disease, especially of the structural and functional changes in tissues and organs of the body that cause or are caused by disease
Dorlands Illustrated Medical Dictionary (25th Edition)

This chapter represents a necessary technical section of this manual. Necessary because it will provide insight into how things work, may go wrong, and how they may be remedied.

Much of the factual information has only been clarified within the last two decades, and even now is only partially complete. We are living through an exhilarating time of dramatic advance in scientific knowledge.

The material that follows is a brief summary of the most important aspects of this information in relation to the reproductive cycle, the hormones that are produced and control the cycle, where and how they work, and what can go wrong. Even scanning this chapter will add to your knowledge. Many readers should find this information provides an exciting glimpse into the unique background of the perpetuation of life itself. Along the way, the concepts of hormones, the glands that produce them, their effects on body tissues and organs, and ultimately the meaning of menopause itself, will become clearer.

The human body is an exquisite mechanism. Every single function inevitably involves many other organs and processes. This is true in part for an automobile, a TV set, or a computer. But they cannot exert full control of themselves, they cannot autoregulate every function necessary for survival, and therein lies the difference.

To understand how something works, you first need to know about its parts. In medicine, the description of the parts is called *anatomy*. How they work is called *physiology*, and *molecular biology* explains the function right down to the tiniest building blocks, the molecules.

THE PARTS – ANATOMY

Early gynecologists, the only doctors at the time interested in any aspect of women's health, usually regarded their specialty starting at the belly button and ending at the top of the thighs. They were, after all, largely surgeons and most medical issues were not on their minds. It was also a way of avoiding things about which very little was known. Over time it became clear that the female monthly cycle was under the control of certain centers in the brain. Their targets were what are called *endocrine glands*.

ENDOCRINE AND EXOCRINE GLANDS

<u>Two types of glands exist in the body</u>:

Exocrine glands, or outside glands, produce and release chemical substances directly onto surfaces. For example, sweat glands on the skin aid in cooling it, and sebaceous glands produce the oily sebum that aids in softening it. They receive their instructions from chemical messengers, and these can include being activated by chemicals in the blood coming from the *endocrine glands*.

Endocrine glands, or inside glands, produce and release substances directly into the blood stream. These substances, or chemical messengers, are called *hormones*.

Signals are sent from and received in the brain. We are all aware of the fact that nerves leave the brain through the spinal cord and get to every part of the body. That system looks like an electric circuit board, with messages able to travel in both directions. But less well known is the fact that the brain has another way of sending out messages and responding to returning signals. That mechanism is through the two-way traffic that travels between the brain centers and the endocrine glands. A little awareness of these higher brain centers that have these hormone-related abilities is a good starting point.

HYPOTHALAMUS:

Virtually in the middle of the skull lies one of the most important endocrine glands. The hypothalamus is to the human body what the ground-control coordinating center is to space flight. It is a small part of the lower surface of the brain and has a shape resembling a funnel.

Impulses or messages reach the hypothalamus from a variety of sources. Signals from the outside senses like sight, smell, hearing, taste, and touch, as well as from inside sources from the rest of the brain, endocrine glands, the nervous system, and so forth, are directed to the hypothalamus. Crucially, this central area of the brain is connected to virtually all the other areas of the brain. The hypothalamus has the uncanny ability to coordinate much of this information.

The hypothalamus makes several hormones. The hypothalamic hormone that is of importance to understanding the monthly cycle is called *gonadotropin-releasing hormone*, which I will refer to as GnRH.

PITUITARY GLAND:

Directly beneath the hypothalamus in a bony cave in the base of the skull lies the pea-sized structure called the *pituitary gland*. It is also an endocrine gland, which means that it too can make hormones. Two of these hormones that are crucial to directing and synchronizing the monthly cycle are called *follicle stimulating hormone* (FSH) and *luteinizing hormone* (LH). Together they are called the *gonadotropins*, and the reason for that will soon become clear.

OVARY:

Most people are surprised to learn that the *ovary* is also an endocrine gland (also called the *female gonad*). The *male gonad* is the *testis*, (also an endocrine gland). There are two ovaries and they have two functions - to produce hormones and eggs. The testis, derived from the same embryonic tissue, produces hormones and sperm.

The process of hormone production and egg release are directly interrelated, and like the old song, "you cannot have one without the other."

The ovaries produce several hormones, of which two are so important to this narrative that they should be regarded as the central characters. Their names are *estrogen* and *progesterone*. The third important character is named *testosterone*, and I will come back to this hormone later. Collectively, all of the above are usually referred to as the *reproductive hormones*. Another important fact is that these three hormones are part of the family called *steroid hormones*. As a subgroup of the steroid family of hormones, estrogen, progesterone, and testosterone are called the *sex steroids*. Steroid describes a molecule with a specific structure.

Before the birth of a female baby there are several million eggs in the two ovaries, but for a completely unknown reason, this number reduces dramatically by birth to about 500,000 remaining eggs. Unlike the male, who is able to produce new spermatozoa for the rest of his life, the female ovary, again for reasons unknown, continues to lose eggs until the supply is virtually exhausted at menopause.

If an ovary, about the size of a large walnut, is cut in half, numerous little structures become visible on the cut surface. What you see is actually dependent on the age of the woman, and if she is still of childbearing age, the stage of the monthly cycle.

Logically, as you would anticipate because human body functions are remarkably coordinated, each of the types of structure that you might see develops from the one before it.

The *primordial follicle* is the early egg surrounded by specific tissue cells. When it is appropriately stimulated it converts into a *Graafian follicle* that produces estrogen in the first two weeks of the average 28-day cycle, and then releases the egg. The Graafian follicle then changes its appearance and function and becomes a yellow spherical structure called the *corpus luteum* (which simply means yellow body). It produces estrogen and progesterone after the egg is released. If pregnancy results from the released egg being fertilized, the corpus luteum will continue to grow and function for at least 3 months as the *corpus luteum of pregnancy*, a vital role in maintaining the early pregnancy. If there is no pregnancy, it will age and shrivel into a *corpus albicans* (which means white body), which is a small, dense, white structure, without any function.

Largely ignored, and most unfortunately so, is the fact that these structures are surrounded by "packing material." This comprises nerve endings, blood vessels, and of tremendous importance, lots of little cells called *stromal cells*. Of relatively little importance before the menopause, they can be of major importance after.

The supporting cells (stromal cells) in the ovary are often discounted as unimportant. But let me arouse your curiosity with the intriguing thought that how they behave after menopause can have a major impact on your future health and life.

THE HYPOTHALAMIC-PITUITARY-OVARIAN AXIS:

In human function, critical to reproduction is the relationship of the parts described above to each other. Collectively we call this the *hypothalamic-pituitary-ovarian axis*. The entire reproductive cycle is controlled through a complex interplay of signals through this axis. More later.

OTHER SEX ORGANS:

The female sex organs are divided into structures on the inside and the outside of the body.

The inner organs are the ovaries, the *uterus* (womb), the *fallopian tubes*, and the *vagina*.

The outer area of the genitalia is called the *vulva*, comprising the *mons pubis* (or mound), the *labia minora* and *labia majora* (the inner and outer lips), and the *clitoris*.

OTHER ORGANS FOUND IN THE PELVIS:

Apart from the sex organs, other organs are found in the pelvis. The *bladder* lies in front of the uterus, and the tube leading from the bladder to the outside is called the *urethra*. It exits just below the clitoris and above the entrance to the vagina, between the vulval labia. The *bowel* lies above and behind the uterus, and the *rectum* (end of the large bowel) and *anus* (opening of the bowel to the exterior), lie behind the vagina.

The relationship of all these organs to the vagina is of importance when we come to consider the problem of *prolapse*, or drop of the pelvic organs. As this is a condition quite likely to start becoming bothersome after menopause, I will return to the subject later.

BREASTS:

The *breasts* are made up of glandular tissue surrounded by fat as a form of packing tissue. The *ducts* from the *glands* end in the nipple. The cell types of the ducts and the secreting parts of the glands are quite different. The function of the breast is not related to size. The important fact to remember about breasts is that, as exocrine glands, they can react to hormones, and also that the glands are the site for cancer when it develops in the breast.

Fibrous bands known as *Cooper's ligaments* run through the packing tissue of the breasts and attach to the firm tissue that lies like a sheet covering the muscle of the chest wall, thus anchoring the breasts to the chest wall.

HOW THE BODY FUNCTIONS

More intriguing even than form is function. How the parts work and integrate has been the subject of considerable research. The more we learn about this, the greater are the opportunities for defining and developing new treatments.

LIFE EVENTS OVER WHICH WE HAVE NO CONTROL

Without entering the debate on the beginnings of life, an individual begins with *fertilization*, that is the joining of the *sperm and the egg*. For the first 8 weeks the conceptus is called the *embryo* because it is still forming organs like heart and lungs. After that it is called the *fetus*, and growth and maturation of organs occurs over the rest of the average 40-week pregnancy.

Birth itself is a landmark, the visible beginning of the human life cycle. Not one of us can predict or know what lies in store for us. But like day follows night, certain events are inevitable. Following birth the baby proceeds through *infancy* and *childhood*. Late childhood, or the "teens" will be marked by a distinct event in girls, the first menstrual period or *menarche*, and the time around this is called *puberty* or *adolescence*. This marks the entrance into the *reproductive age* of the female, and will continue until the final menstrual period or *menopause*. The time related events around the menopause are usually collectively named the climacteric or *perimenopause*. The years beyond menopause, *postmenopause*, merge into the *senium*, or old age, only to be eventually and inevitably terminated by *death*.

While all the above events are inevitable except if a tragedy of premature death occurs, advances in medical science, supported by a direct effort on your part, can have a positive impact on this life cycle. In other words, life can be prolonged, and of more importance, the quality of that life can be improved.

HOW HORMONES WORK

The steroid hormones estrogen, progesterone, and testosterone, should be regarded as keys to specific locks. As they circulate through the body, they are testing all the locks in all the different cell types and body organs searching for a perfect fit. The locks are called *receptors*, and these vary. For example there are at least two kinds of estrogen-receptor (ER), ER-alpha and ER-beta. Opening one will potentially have quite different effects to opening another. The hormone-receptor combination triggers gene-related actions.

More ER-alpha is found in the reproductive system, that is, in uterus and breast; more ER-beta is found in the other tissues, like brain, bone, blood vessels, and lung. This information should alert you to the fact that the discovery of this difference opened a whole new world of potential medications developed to act selectively on one or other of these receptors.

THE PRODUCTION OF HORMONES DURING THE REPRODUCTIVE YEARS

It is not an exaggeration to say that the reproductive cycle, also called the menstrual or ovulatory cycle, is the key to creation itself. The ebb and flow of hormone production is not only associated with the release of an egg. The fluctuating hormone levels also have direct effects on virtually every body organ and function, from mood to bone development, and from sex drive to cardiovascular health.

The following description of the female reproductive cycle is such an amazing series of events, the yin and yang of life, that I offer little excuse for describing the way it flows.

Each reproductive cycle commences with the first day of the period (day 1). At that point all the reproductive hormone levels are low. Low levels of circulating reproductive hormones remind the hypothalamus that there was a failure to achieve a pregnancy in the previous cycle, and that it is time to initiate the process all over again with a new ovulatory cycle. The hypothalamus accordingly sends a burst of its hormone messenger GnRH to the pituitary gland. The pituitary, sitting dormant and waiting for the call, releases the FSH, and what follows is why it is named follicle-stimulating hormone.

The FSH travels through the blood stream and when it reaches the ovary it stimulates a primordial follicle to start maturing and grow into a Graafian follicle. The Graafian follicle in turn produces increasing amounts of estrogen until it reaches a peak level at day 14, the middle of the reproductive cycle. That high level of estrogen travelling though the blood to the brain carries the message to the hypothalamus that the follicle is ripe and ready to release its egg. The hypothalamus immediately sends another GnRH message to the pituitary gland, and in turn the pituitary pours LH into the blood circulation. LH has the power to stimulate the follicle to release its captive egg, called *ovulation*, and then for the follicle to convert into the corpus luteum. The corpus luteum is able to make estrogen and progesterone for nearly 14 days without any reminders from head office.

Now one of two things can happen:

1. If a sperm fertilizes the egg, and the resultant embryo successfully implants itself into the lining of the uterus, the cells from the conceptus that attach to the uterus and eventually become the placenta will produce a new hormone called *human chorionic gonadotropin* (HCG). The remarkable thing about HCG is that it has the same effect as LH. In other words, if pregnancy is successfully achieved, the pregnancy itself produces a hormone that keeps the corpus luteum functioning for nearly 3 months, and producing ever-increasing amounts of estrogen and progesterone. This is truly amazing. The embryo creates its own signal for early life support! Eventually the placenta will produce enough of all the hormones needed to maintain a successful pregnancy, and the corpus luteum of pregnancy will shrivel into a corpus albicans.

2. If fertilization does not occur, the corpus luteum will produce estrogen and progesterone, peaking at about day 21 (called the *luteal maximum*), and then will gradually decrease its ability to sustain itself. By day 27 to 28 the corpus luteum runs out of steam, transforms into a corpus albicans, produces very little estrogen and progesterone, and that signal gets back to the hypothalamus which is prompted to try all over again with another reproductive cycle.

WHAT HAS THIS TO DO WITH MENOPAUSE?

The take-home lesson from all of the above is that there is a constant, albeit cyclic, ability of the ovary to produce estrogen and progesterone throughout the reproductive years. What these hormones actually do around the body is explained below.

The real issue is that after menopause the cyclic production of estrogen and progesterone from the ovary ceases. Remember, the ovary is presented before birth with all the eggs it will ever have, and no new ones will ever be formed again. Following some 35 years of regular menstrual cycles, interrupted only by any pregnancies and breast feeding that may have occurred, the ovary runs out of its supply of eggs. The hormonal changes are truly dramatic.

I am often asked if taking birth control pills results in saving eggs. Unfortunately, the answer is no. Even on the pill, there is a constant loss of eggs. The difference is that the pill blocks any one follicle from reaching maturity and releasing an egg.

As the ovaries run out of follicles, the hypothalamus goes into overtime, sending increasing amounts of GnRH to the pituitary. The pituitary in turn works harder and harder sending increasing amounts of FSH into the bloodstream and hence to the ovary. The ovary is just unable to respond. Very occasionally, one final follicle with an egg may accept the FSH signal, and a *breakthrough ovulation* may occur. When the ovary has failed to do even that, and 12 months have gone by without ovulation and a period, the official diagnosis of menopause can be made.

SO WHAT IS SO IMPORTANT ABOUT THE SEX STEROIDS?

The sex steroids have a major impact on the structure and function of virtually every body tissue and organ. This is best explained by considering their effect on the most important of these tissues and organs.

As we go through this list, take into consideration of what was mentioned earlier about different tissues having different receptors to the estrogen.

DIRECT EFFECTS ON THE SEX ORGANS BEFORE MENOPAUSE:

Think of the sex steroids as being building contractors. Estrogen is a growth-promoting hormone. In the building analogy, it would be responsible for building the basic structure of a house, that is, the walls, floor, roof, and so on. Progesterone is the decorator, putting in carpets, light fittings, furniture, ornaments, and the rest. Just as a decorator would have nothing to do if the house was not built, progesterone would likewise be jobless if the tissues had not first been primed by estrogen.

Vulva: Before puberty, the vulva of a child has a flat slit-like appearance with tiny labia. With the onset of production of sex steroids at puberty these tissues undergo a dramatic change. The first event is the appearance of hair on the mons pubis, and this is followed by an increase in the size of the labia, and a slight increase in the size of the clitoris.

Vagina: Estrogen stimulates growth and thickening of the vaginal lining. The real effect is an increase in the thickness, pliability, and potential sex function of the vagina.

Uterus: The lining of the uterus, named the *endometrium*, thickens during the first half of the reproductive cycle,

32

stimulated by estrogen. This is therefore called the *proliferative phase*, and the lining at this time has a classic appearance under the microscope, called the *proliferative endometrium*. In the second half of the cycle, progesterone, the decorator, converts the proliferative endometrium into the *secretory endometrium*. What has happened is that the progesterone has prepared the lining to be a welcoming place for a fertilized egg to move into. In unsuccessful cycles, the levels of estrogen and progesterone fall, the endometrium shrinks, and then begins to break away. Thus appears the period, or *menstrual flow*. These hormone effects will occur irrespective of whether the hormone comes from the ovary itself, or a woman is taking hormones as medication. Too much estrogen will cause too much thickening of the endometrium, and this can result in abnormal bleeding patterns.

Breasts: Many women feel changes in their breasts during their normal monthly cycle. This too is the result of the changing level of the sex hormones. These symptoms are usually most marked in the second half of the cycle. Here what is happening is that estrogen only increases the size of the ducts in the first half of the cycle. Progesterone, the decorator, stimulates the breast glands during the second half of the cycle to get ready to produce milk in the event of a possible pregnancy. But the role of progesterone in the breast is different in that it stimulates both growth and development during this process.

EFFECTS ON THE REST OF THE BODY:

The sex steroids impact every organ and bodily function. Consequently, after menopause, their reduced levels will have many possible negative effects on body tissues and functions.

Consider an automobile getting older and running out of oil. Parts that have been subject to wear and tear are now also no longer lubricated. Occasionally something will give in and break.

Some of the important areas affected are listed below. I will explain the impact on these tissues in the following chapter where I address the critical question – "What are the true effects of menopause?"

1. Skin
2. Body weight
3. Hair
4. Vision
5. Hearing
6. Muscles
7. Joints
8. Skeleton (bone)
9. Teeth
10. Heart and blood vessels
11. Brain function – body temperature control, sleep, mood, and memory
12. Sexual behavior
13. Headache
14. Voice

This is quite an impressive list. Alteration of hormonal effects can change function to such an extent that serious symptoms or disease can result.

While paying attention to all that follows, please do not get overly concerned. Firstly, not everyone gets everything. Secondly, I will be clearly showing you how many of these nasty and negative changes can be avoided or ameliorated by a combination of healthy living practices, supplements, and if appropriate, medications.

CHAPTER 4

THE TRUE EFFECTS OF MENOPAUSE

Life and body functions do not occur in isolation. Ovarian function and ultimately its failure after menopause is after all only one of all the body organs and functions that are aging. This creates one of the most difficult challenges in medical research – to separate the coexisting effects of aging on body function and disease development from the true and direct effects of the reduction in sex steroid production by the ovary.

There is yet another monumental challenge: to determine whether those effects that have been demonstrated to be directly related to menopause can be reversed by some form of hormonal treatment. It cannot be simply taken for granted that prescribing hormones can automatically reverse symptoms or disease processes initiated by loss of hormones with menopause.

In this chapter, I summarize the true effects of menopause and will also attempt to differentiate the role of aging itself in diseases that may develop at the same time.

So let me to get on with my first task, answering that key question "What are the true effects of menopause?"

The best way of answering this crucial question is to systematically go through the parts of the body and explain what we know about each. Through this process, in this and the next chapter, I will then differentiate between:

- *The true early effects and potential symptoms*
- *The late-presenting problems*

TRUE MENOPAUSE-RELATED EFFECTS

SEX ORGAN CHANGES AFTER MENOPAUSE

OVARIES: Earlier I described how eggs run out at menopause and the ability of the ovary to make estrogen and progesterone follows suit. I also alluded to the packing cells (*stromal cells*). Something I have found both intriguing and a source of regret, because so little research has been dedicated to the stromal cells, is how they may change after menopause. In some women, they become fewer and fewer, and the postmenopausal ovary shrivels into a small whitish organ resembling a firm acorn. As you would expect, it has very little activity or function. But in many other women, the opposite happens. The stromal cells increase in size and number, a process called *hypertrophy* and *hyperplasia*, and their cellular chemical activity increases. Indeed, that ovary remains much the same size and consistency as before the menopause.

What is most amazing about this second type of ovary is that it continues to be an active endocrine gland. But instead of producing the female sex steroids, it produces male hormone (androgens). Now consider another intriguing piece of scientific information. The ability of the body to convert male hormone into estrogen increases with both increasing body weight and with age. As aging is inevitable, and most women

38

gradually increase their bodyweight as they get older, the result is an extraordinary situation that I call a *compensatory effect.*

This compensatory effect in summary is an ovary that has transformed itself into a gland that has changed its function, developing the ability to produce a precursor to estrogen, namely, an androgen. With the body's increasing ability to convert the androgen to estrogen, the result is a sort of self-regulation in which a new source for estrogen has been developed. This may actually explain the remarkably different way different women respond to menopause, and whether they need hormone treatment or not. This information should begin to plant the seed in your mind as to why I subtitled this book "One size does not fit all."

VAGINA: Withdrawal of estrogen eventually leads to marked thinning of the vaginal lining, a condition called *vaginal atrophy.* For the woman who is not sexually active, this may have little consequence; indeed she is highly unlikely to be aware that she has it. Unfortunately, with the thinning of the vaginal lining, there are fewer of the surface cells to shed. Before menopause, these cells produce a sugar called *glycogen,* and the normal vaginal flora thrives on this. As they consume it, they make the vagina slightly acidic and this keeps out foreign invaders like yeast and certain bacteria. So the postmenopausal vagina is more susceptible to infections, a condition called *atrophic vaginitis.* This condition can present with itching, burning, vaginal discharge, and vaginal pain. The sexually active woman has a greater problem, as the thin vaginal lining can be a source of pain during intercourse, a condition called *dyspareunia.*

VULVA: After menopause, there is a loss of pubic hair and the labia shrink in size. The opening to the vagina, the introitus, narrows in the absence of regular sexual activity, and heterosexual women becoming sexually active after a time of abstinence can suffer pain and difficulty with penetration.

UTERUS: Initially, the on-again off-again production of hormones will cause menstrual periods to be irregular, and flow can increase or decrease compared to the past. This time is often referred to as the perimenopause. Ultimately, the periods stop, which is, of course, menopause. Loss of periods is called *amenorrhea* in medical terminology.

PELVIC FLOOR AND URINARY TRACT: The bony pelvis is like a basin without a bottom. The bottom of this bony pelvis is closed by one of the most remarkable systems in our bodies. The *pelvic floor* is a muscular diaphragm that attaches all around the base of the bony pelvis.

In four-legged animals, the abdominal wall supports the weight of all the abdominal contents. When our ancestors decided to stand erect so that they could look for their prey over longer distances, much of our body dynamics changed. The muscular diaphragm plugging the bottom of the bony pelvis was instantly required to support everything contained above.

The Achilles' Heel of this system is the necessity for openings in the muscular diaphragm through which the bladder, vagina, and rectum could reach the outside. That is, these openings could be a problem in plugging the pelvis.

First problem is labor and delivery – a large baby has to get out through a small aperture that as a result can become stretched and damaged. Next, the pelvic diaphragm is under the influence of hormones, so withdrawal after menopause can result in the diaphragm becoming weaker, thinner, and more flaccid. Together with tissue aging, the bladder can weigh down and bulge through the top wall of the vagina (which after all does also function as the floor of the urinary bladder). This stretched bulge is called a *cystocele*. Alternately, with the bottom wall of the vagina being the roof of the rectum, a bulge from that direction is called a *rectocele*. Even the uterus itself may drop and this is called *uterine prolapse*. In many women, even if present altogether or individually, there may be few or no symptoms. In others there may be a sensation of something dropping or falling out.

Postmenopausal changes in the *bladder*, and the pipe passing through the pelvic diaphragm, the *urethra*, may also cause symptoms. These include leaking bladder (*urinary incontinence*) and urgency to empty the bladder (*overactive bladder OAB*). These postmenopause-related events are not an inevitable result of aging, and should not be considered to be a normal part of menopause.

Urinary incontinence is leaking that occurs without a sense of urge to actually pass water. Coughing, sneezing, muscular exertion, and even walking or running can cause the bladder to leak. Whether menopause makes this condition worse is debatable. OAB, sometimes called *urge incontinence,* is quite different. There is a sudden intense urge to urinate followed by uncontrolled leaking that can be quite large in amount. Even worse can be a combination of both stress and urge!

BREASTS: Menopause is not associated with an increased risk of breast cancer. If anything, the rate of increase slows after menopause. In fact, early menopause before age 40 has a lower risk of breast cancer. Aging is the biggest risk factor.

The Cooper's ligaments in the breast that connect them to the chest wall are made of collagen and some muscle fibers. The collagen decreases after menopause, and the ligaments stretch. This has been called *Cooper's Droop* because it may be the main factor that is responsible for the breasts hanging lower, or drooping, with age. Doubtless, gravity also takes its toll with time, as it does on skin all over the body.

MENOPAUSE EFFECTS ELSEWHERE IN THE BODY

SKIN: The skin actually ages remarkably well, with sun exposure producing much worse effects; compare areas on your body typically exposed to the sun with those areas that are always covered. But the hormones do have a significant role. There is strong evidence that estrogen loss has a far greater negative impact on skin than aging. One-third of the supporting matrix of skin (*collagen*) is lost in the first 5 years after menopause. This also occurs in collagen all over the body. The reduction of estrogen also thins the layers of skin cells.

Dry skin (Xerosis) and *wrinkling* are the most common problems with aging skin. Estrogen is a stimulator of the sebaceous glands. So aging and estrogen deprivation in combination will result in less blood flow to the skin, loss of the supporting fibers (collagen), and thinning of the skin cell layers. These together with the loss of sebaceous gland secretion produce dry skin that can be easily traumatized or bruised. Wrinkling is the other effect, particularly as the collagen is lost. The skin can get a sort of crinkled paper appearance from all this. Deeper wrinkles are largely due to age and gravity. Smoking accelerates skin aging.

Testosterone normally stimulates both the oil-producing glands (*sebaceous glands*) of the skin and the hair follicles. Remember the ovarian stromal cell compensatory effect I described earlier? As androgen levels become relatively higher than estrogen after menopause in those women with that ovarian change, the result can be *acne* and *hair growth*. Consequently, many women after menopause find a greater growth of hair on the upper lip, chin, and sideburn areas. This is perfectly normal.

Another important skin change results from estrogen's effect on the sensory nerves in the skin - the higher the amount of estrogen, the more sensitive the skin. After menopause, this *reduction of sensation* can be felt in different ways. I have had patients tell me "my clothes don't feel the same on me as they used to." Others tell me, "I don't get the same sensation when my partner touches me." In other words, the reduced skin sensation can have a negative impact on sexual response.

BODY WEIGHT: "Menopause makes you fat" is the commonest complaint heard in the clinician's office. True or false?

In fact, menopause is associated with a loss of muscle mass and an increase in fat mass. Significantly, muscle is heavier than fat. The increased fat tends to gather in the abdominal cavity and waist region, as well as around the hips. So although technically there is no direct increase in weight caused by menopause, the change in body shape is what worries women most, and is often perceived as weight gain.

Here is an interesting observation. As men age and lose testosterone, they too lose muscle and gain fat in the abdominal region. It is almost as if men and women, unless they take effective preventive steps, begin to get a similar body shape as they age.

The critically important thing to know is that as body weight and fat mass increase, so does the likelihood of serious adverse consequences. These include cardiovascular disease, high blood pressure (*hypertension*), mature onset diabetes (*type 2 diabetes*), some cancers, arthritis, and premature death. Gaining just 15 to 20 pounds significantly increases the risk of a heart attack (*myocardial infarction*) in the future. Better news is that a loss of just 10% of body weight by overweight women results in multiple health benefits – less diabetes, heart attacks, and hypertension.

Given that over 65% of women ages 45 to 55 are overweight in the United States, here lies an enormous opportunity for improvement in health.

HAIR: There are hair changes after menopause; some directly related to the altered hormonal environment, but age, genes, and other factors also play a role.

The tendency toward the predominance of male hormone over female hormone could account for *growth* on the lip, sideburns, and elsewhere on the body, as well as *loss* in the form of mild male pattern baldness. The latter is most likely to manifest as some loss on the crown and there may be slight recession at the temples.

Estrogen is known to stimulate hair growth, and even more important, to reduce loss. Reduced sebaceous gland secretion results in dry hair.

Hair changes can influence feelings about body image, and if a cause of concern should be part of the discussion with your clinician.

VISION: Menopause and aging both affect vision. After menopause, there may be any or all of the following – *dry eye*, need for reading glasses (*presbyopia*), *cataracts*, *glaucoma* (increased pressure in the eyes), *retinal detachment*, and possibly even *macular degeneration*. Aging and sun damage are the most likely cause of the cataracts. There is good evidence that estrogen loss is associated with dry eye and macular degeneration.

An eye exam is obviously essential around the time of menopause, even if your vision has been perfect until that time.

HEARING: Hearing too is related to menopause and aging. Menopause appears to accelerate hearing loss (*presbycusis*).

MUSCLES: Muscle loss is a natural part of aging and can be accelerated by loss of estrogen. The slight increase in male hormone in some women can play a protective role. But, here is a great model for "Use it or lose it!" A good exercise program started and maintained from any age can really avoid this problem.

I am often asked if *fibromyalgia* is related to menopause. This is a condition characterized by chronic, persistent, sometimes intermittent, pain in the muscles and joints. The answer is, unfortunately, no. I say unfortunately because it means that hormone treatments have not proven effective.

JOINTS: Our joints get quite a beating during life, and aging and our early activities will clearly have an ultimate cost. The commonest inflammatory joint disease is *osteoarthritis*, also called *degenerative arthritis*. Almost everyone gets some of this with aging. The joints that tend most to wear out are the knees, hips, spinal bones (*vertebrae*) in the neck and low back, and feet. Women and men are equally affected, so this is not a "menopause thing." The aggravating factors are really overuse (high impact sports, for example), and injury.

The next most common type of arthritis is *rheumatoid arthritis*. Although three out of four cases occur in women, there does not appear to be a relationship to menopause.

SKELETON (BONE): Here is one part of the body that is dramatically impacted by hormones. I always quote a question I once heard a friend of mine's 12-year-old son ask him: "Dad, why are grandmas always so short?" Let me explain why.

If you have ever seen or felt a real skeleton, the thought must cross your mind that bone is a pretty permanent substance;

once developed, never changing. This is just so far from the truth. Like every other part of the body, bone is dynamic. It is constantly renewing itself in a process called *bone remodeling*.

Bone remodeling is a delicate balancing act. As bone ages, it becomes brittle, and brittle bones break more easily. The body needs to get rid of the brittle bone and replace it with new strong and flexible bone. This balance is maintained by a process that has to take out the old bone (*bone resorption*) and replace it with new bone (*bone deposition*).

As a child grows, there is a heavy emphasis on building new bone. Under normal circumstances, this positive balance of more bone deposition than resorption will go on into the late 20s and early 30s when the individual reaches *peak bone mass*. This is a time when we have the most bone in the bank twe will ever have. The amount of bone will be determined by many factors including genes, sex (men have more bone than women), diet (good protein, calcium, mineral and vitamin intake), vitamin D, exercise and activity, and so forth.

After a plateau in middle age, the balance begins to go the other way, and aging is associated with losing more bone than making it. If this negative balance goes too far, so much bone is lost that it now has the risk of breaking (*fractures*), and we call this condition of abnormal low bone mass or bone thinning *osteoporosis*.

Both men and women lose bone as they age. Risk factors that increase the likelihood of developing osteoporosis include family history, sex, race, age of menopause, diet and nutrition, smoking and alcohol abuse, taking corticosteroid drugs such as for asthma, and chronic diseases, for example of the kidney or thyroid.

Women are unfortunately at greater risk of developing osteoporosis for a number of reasons:

1. They start with less bone in the bank than men.
2. They are the stronger sex and live longer, giving more time for the gradual loss with aging to accumulate.
3. Estrogen plays a key role in preventing bone loss. The reduction of estrogen at menopause results in a few years of *rapid bone loss* – in 5 to 7 years, up to 10% of the skeletal bone mass can disappear.

Brittle osteoporotic bone is more likely to break. This can result from a fall, or from something as simple as a bump in the road. More than half of American women over 50 demonstrate bone loss – over one-third will eventually have problems. Postmenopausal osteoporosis is associated with over a quarter million hip fractures a year, costing our health system over 15 billion dollars every year. But the real cost is in human terms – one in two women will lose independent living after a hip fracture and a quarter of those will never leave nursing institutions; 10% die within 12 months.

The spinal bones (*vertebra*) can break silently. What happens is that any extra pressure on the weakened bones results in them compressing or crushing. Simply stepping off a sidewalk could do this. As the vertebrae crush, the spine curves forward and the result may be the so-called "dowagers hump." Not only does this drop the bottom of the rib cage in front lower toward the top of the pelvic bone, giving a bulge of the stomach, but it also results in loss of height – thereby giving the answer to the question posed by my friend's son.

Unfortunately, crush fractures of the vertebrae can also be associated with terrible back pain. This can be so severe as to literally immobilize a woman, and in many instances is the difference between independent living and moving into an institution.

This human tragedy following fractures of the hip and spine is largely preventable. There have been huge strides in our knowledge about the problem, and several families of new drugs have been developed to prevent or treat established osteoporosis. All about this later...

TEETH: The jaws are bone, and teeth are really a kind of specialized bone. Tooth loss after menopause results from atrophy (shrinkage) of the bony tooth sockets. This in turn leads to retraction of the gums, the nonenamel part of the teeth getting exposed, and bacterial invasion of little pockets that open up around the teeth. Indeed, women with severe osteoporosis are three times more likely to have no teeth than unaffected women.

Prevention of bone loss after menopause is truly necessary for good dental health.

HEART AND BLOOD VESSELS: At the outset of describing the number one cause of death in aging women, we need to understand the terminology:

Cardiovascular disease (CVD): This is an umbrella term that includes all heart disease, hypertension, stroke, and some diseases of the blood vessels.

Coronary heart disease (CHD): Disease of the blood vessels feeding the heart can cause heart attacks (*myocardial infarction*) and heart-related chest pain (*angina pectoris*).

Venous thrombo-embolism (VTE): Blood clots forming in the leg or pelvic veins can break off and be carried to the lungs. Here the clot blocks an oxygen-carrying artery to a part of the lung, which is then starved of oxygen and nutrients and the segment of lung essentially dies (*infarction*).

Atherosclerosis: The accumulation of fat-like plaques in the wall of an artery, a disease called *atheromatosis*, can lead to atherosclerosis, which is a diseased and narrowed artery. If an artery that feeds the heart (coronary artery) becomes blocked, the result will be a heart attack. In the brain this would result in a stroke.

There are many factors that contribute to the development and progression of the above problems. But it is now beyond doubt that the female hormones play a significant role. Early loss of ovarian function results in increased risk of CVD. Given the rapid advances in knowledge about all of this, we are now at a point where the most frequent cause of death and disability in older women can actually be reduced. This is something that offers great hope.

The development of CVD is complex, and certainly there are many factors that contribute to this. The following are the key risk factors:

General Risk Factors

1. Abnormal blood fat levels, particularly cholesterol
2. High blood pressure (hypertension)
3. Diabetes
4. Obesity
5. Cigarette smoking
6. Poor diet
7. Physical inactivity
8. Family history of stroke or heart disease

Women-only Risk Factors

1. Early menopause, before age 45
2. Surgical menopause
3. Oral contraceptive use
4. Low levels of estrogen
5. Starting hormone therapy 10 years after menopause

As complex as this may appear, these lists, and how we can approach the prevention and treatment of many of these factors, give great cause for hope.

The normally functioning ovary during the reproductive years obviously offers some protection against the development of vascular disease and all its subsequent negative outcomes like heart attacks and stroke.

If you closely consider the items in the two lists above, you will realize that we could mix and match them into two other lists that classify them in a quite different way:

Unavoidable Risk Factors

1. Family history (your genes)
2. Age of menopause
3. Susceptibility to increased cholesterol
4. Hypertension
5. Diabetes

Potentially Alterable Risk Factors

1. Abnormal blood fat levels, particularly cholesterol
2. High blood pressure (hypertension)
3. Diabetes
4. Obesity
5. Cigarette smoking
6. Poor diet
7. Physical inactivity
8. Surgical menopause
9. Low levels of estrogen
10. Starting HT more than 10 years after menopause
11. Oral contraceptives

Intriguing? Clearly, more factors are actually within your control to reduce your risk of heart attack, stroke, and the negative impact they may have on duration and quality of life.

BRAIN FUNCTION – BODY TEMPERATURE CONTROL, SLEEP, MOOD, MEMORY: The brain is a sponge for hormones that in turn exert a multiplicity of effects. When present in normal amounts the sex steroids can trigger specific brain actions – when absent this ability is reduced or lost.

While many of these processes and conditions interact with each other, I will consider specific conditions one by one:

Body Temperature Control: Sudden short-lived wide fluctuations in body temperature are the hallmark of menopause. Whether called *hot flushes, hot flashes, night sweats,* or their technical name *vasomotor symptoms (VMS),* they and their impact are the same. An episode of flushing, sometimes preceded by an early warning flash, is associated with a sensation varying from warmth to intense heat on the upper body and face. Perspiration follows as the body attempts to counteract by cooling, and as the perspiration evaporates, so there can actually be chilling and shivering. When these events occur during the night, they can disrupt sleep and are called night sweats. They can last up to 5 or 6 minutes or more, and are associated with remarkable temperature increases, as well as the heart beating rapidly (*palpitations*). They can be infrequent (weekly or monthly) or frequent (hourly). Reaction to them can vary from being a minor nuisance, all the way to a total disruptive influence on regular activities and living.

The second most common symptom of menopause after irregular periods, 75% of women are affected by VMS. This is a true "rule of quarters." One quarter of women are not affected at all. Mild, moderate, or severe VMS, each account for a quarter of women. VMS can start several years before menopause and usually begin to decline in frequency and severity 2-3 years after menopause. Unfortunately, they do persist in some women for many years.

We do not know the cause of VMS – it is currently a "syndrome of theories." They occur more frequently in African-American women, followed by Hispanic, Caucasian, Chinese, and Japanese women. Of greater influence than race is body mass index (BMI). The greater the BMI, the higher the prevalence of VMS.

Those women who have early onset of menopause as a result of surgical removal of the ovaries, chemotherapy, or radiotherapy, are more likely to have the most severe form of VMS.

Never to be forgotten is that there are other causes for VMS. These include an overactive thyroid gland, epilepsy, hypertension, leukemia, and hormone-producing tumors such as of the adrenal gland and appendix. Certain drugs may also be the cause.

SLEEP: Almost half of women over 50 experience sleep disturbances. These women suffer more frequent insomnia, nighttime awakenings, and are more than twice as likely than younger women to use prescription drugs for sleep. Poor sleep or disrupted sleep in turn is associated with symptoms like morning fatigue, irritability, lethargy, inability to concentrate, a perceived loss of memory, difficulty in performing tasks, and lack of motivation. The million dollar question is whether nighttime VMS are responsible for the sleep disruption, and what is called the *"snow-ball effect"* of triggering all or some of the above symptoms.

Quality of sleep does vary during the night. Estrogen has been demonstrated to positively influence the good-quality sleep called rapid eye-movement (REM) sleep, which tends to occur during the second half of the night.

There is evidence that after menopause, more women experience sleep-disordered breathing (*SDB, or sleep apnea/hypopnea syndrome*). This can manifest with loud snoring, sleep arousals, and episodes of reduced breathing (hypopnea) or even no breathing (apnea) and reduction in circulating oxygen.

MOOD: The impact of menopause and hormones on sense of well-being and mood has been a subject of my own intense research interest since my days as a young investigator. My initial studies demonstrated a direct effect among ovarian function, hormones, and mood. I am not referring to a major depression, but what we describe as "blue moods" (technically referred to as *dysphoria*). Studies over the years have confirmed these findings, and this mood-elevating effect of estrogen appears to go beyond the snowball effect of eliminating night sweats and disrupted sleep. In addition, compared with women before menopause, perimenopausal women who seek help for mood changes have been found to be less healthy, have more hot flashes and psychosomatic complaints, and even to have suffered more from *premenstrual syndrome* (PMS).

MEMORY: Women around the age of menopause, when surveyed for their greatest health concern, overwhelmingly say breast cancer. However, women over 60 overwhelmingly worry more about memory loss and eventually succumbing to Alzheimer's disease. I guess it is what you see most among your direct peers that influences thinking most. But memory (*cognition*) is a concern for most people as they age (I know it bothers me!).

This word *cognition* has deep meaning, incorporating multiple brain skills including memory, learning ability, powers of concentration, language, spatial abilities, and judgment. There are many factors that can influence each and any of these domains, including physical health, stress, mood, fatigue, drugs and medications, alcohol, and the list is almost endless. As a result it is extremely difficult to determine the role of menopause and hormones for their true effect on cognition. Fortunately, some great minds in the research world are concentrating their efforts into this extremely relevant area of quality of life.

The steroid hormones - and remember this includes estrogen, progesterone, testosterone, and the adrenal hormone *cortisone* – directly influence brain function through receptors in many specific areas of the brain. At this time, there is no firm evidence that menopause negatively affects any of the cognitive skills. Some weak associations have been shown, but these are more likely to be related to mood or aging than to menopause itself.

What about that form of advanced cognition loss called *dementia* in which there is such a disruption of intellectual abilities that usual daily activities become substantially impaired? This sad state may be preceded by a time of moderate cognitive difficulty called *mild cognitive impairment*. Alzheimer's accounts for half of all dementia, with more women affected than men. But that may be because women live longer than men, meaning there are more older women than men. Vascular disease is also a major cause of dementia. Ovarian function does have an impact on vascular health or disease. But at this time we do not have enough evidence to confirm a role of menopause itself as a cause of Alzheimer's disease.

SEXUAL BEHAVIOUR: I address sex in detail later, but we know that the direct effects of menopause on sexual function occur at multiple levels. The brain first and foremost will initiate desire and arousal. Sexual desire (libido) decreases with age in both sexes, and the causes are numerous and variable between individuals. Distressing sexual problems peak between ages 45 and 65, with almost half of American women reporting their existence.

I have already referred to the loss of skin sensation associated with menopause, with negative effects on the nervous system occurring both in the brain and peripherally. For example, there may be less clitoral or vulval sensation.

Finally, the integrity and health of the vagina itself was also explained earlier. With vaginal thinning, intercourse may cause pain and discomfort. The advent of the erectile dysfunction drugs like Viagra certainly did not help the woman with vaginal atrophy, and following their introduction I experienced a rush of older women into the office asking for help. Because their vaginal thinning caused pain, they were not prepared to deal with the changed circumstances.

I will return to all this later.

HEADACHE: Headache is a very common midlife complaint. Of the three kinds of headache, tension, cluster, and migraine, it is the latter that mostly drives people to the doctor's office. Fortunately most headaches are not serious, which is not to minimize the negative impact they can have on quality of life, but some may indicate a more major underlying problem. A trigger mechanism can be identified in many cases, including various foods, stress, and environmental factors like noise or changes in the barometric pressure.

Ovarian hormones, however, affect one type of migraine. While there is no sex-related difference in incidence of headaches before puberty or after menopause, women between 25 and 55 have triple the number of headaches (18% vs. 6%). These headaches occur largely around periods, hence their being named *menstrual migraine*. These headaches may increase in severity during perimenopause, but usually wane after menopause.

VOICE: Remarkably, menopause does affect the vocal chords. This is probably caused by the relative increase in male hormone. The *voice deepens*. While of little importance to most women, it is a problem for women who sing for a living. Most sopranos are no longer able to hit the high notes after menopause. It was probably no coincidence that Beverly Sills retired when she was around 50.

SUMMING THIS ALL UP – CONDITIONS ASSOCIATED WITH MENOPAUSE

I promised to summarize all this for you into:

- *The true early effects and potential symptoms*
- *The late-presenting problems*

The following summary list of conditions associated with menopause is the worst-case scenario – *it is not inevitable that all this will happen to you.*

SITE	PATHOLOGY	SYMPTOMS
Vulva/Vagina	Vaginal atrophy Vaginitis (infections)	Itching, burning Discharge Painful intercourse
Uterus	Utero-vaginal prolapse	Dropping sensation Difficult intercourse
Bladder/Urethra	Altered urethra Infections	Stress incontinence Overactive bladder Urgency & frequency
Skin	Atrophy Androgen effect	Dry skin Easily injured Wrinkles Decreased sensation Acne
Bodyweight	Hormonal effects	Less muscle More fat Increased weight
Hair		Male pattern loss Hair on face Dryness
Vision	Macular degeneration	Dry eye Loss of vision
Hearing		Impaired hearing
Muscles	Reduced mass	Weakness

		Less balance
Joints		No known menopause effect
Headache		Less migraine
Skeleton (bone)	Increased resorption and decreased formation	Osteoporosis Fractures – hip, spine Backache
Teeth	Jaw resorption	Tooth loss Gingivitis
Heart and Blood vessels	Atherosclerosis	Angina pectoris Heart attack Stroke
Brain		VMS – hot flashes Blue moods Disturbed sleep
Sexual behavior		Painful intercourse Reduced desire Reduced sensation
Breasts		Shrinking Sagging
Voice	Androgen effect	Voice deepens

All these potential changes in the different body parts will develop at different rates. Usually these changes are only very slowly progressive, and the onset of symptoms may take years to appear. Of course they may never happen!

Other symptoms may occur very early.

What the real early and late symptoms are, and why the menopause experience is so variable for different women, is where we go next...

CHAPTER 5

WHY EVERYONE'S MENOPAUSE DIFFERS

It should now come as no surprise that the only genuine *early symptoms* directly related to the reduction in sex hormones in the few years around menopause *are in fact remarkably few*! This is the complete list of possible early symptoms:

- ❖ Irregular, missed, heavy or light periods
- ❖ VMS – hot flashes, night sweats, and perspiration
- ❖ Dry eyes

That's it. So what, you may well ask, about all those awful symptoms listed on the grocery list of menopause problems that you find on the websites or in books and magazines trying to sell you miraculous remedies? Hype and marketing? To a large extent yes. So next you will argue, a lot of women complain about a lot of things during and after menopause. Are they imagining all this? The answer is no, but this is going to take a little explaining.

Humans are really complex beings. How we behave, how we react to various situations, what diseases we get, even how those diseases present and progress, are all the result of an interaction between some very special controlling factors.

Each of three interrelated factors influences how we respond to various situations including, in this instance, the menopause. For one person, one factor may have a stronger impact than another. But we are always affected by the following:

- HORMONES
- PSYCHOLOGICAL – internal environment
- SOCIOCULTURAL – external environment

I will expand a little on each to show you how they relate to each other, and what this means for symptoms after menopause. In some women the hormonal effects may override the other effects. In others the psychological makeup or the sociocultural factors may have a stronger impact than the hormonal.

I will occasionally use the term *menopause syndrome*. A syndrome is simply the medical term for a cluster of several symptoms occurring together in relation to a disease or event.

HORMONES – THE SPECIFIC TRUE HORMONE-RELATED SYMPTOMS

Intensive research on several continents has all reached the same remarkable conclusion: the actual true *early symptoms* **directly** resulting from the hormonal changes around menopause are remarkably few. As already indicated, these are:

1. Menstrual irregularities
2. Vasomotor symptoms – hot flashes, night sweats
3. Dry eye

Later symptoms may result from the changes that occur in various parts of the body, as described in the previous chapter. As the severity of these changes and the rate at which they develop are so variable, the potential for an actual problem will be quite different for different women. A few examples of the potential organ changes and their possible late-onset symptoms include the following:

1. Vaginal thinning causing pain with intercourse
2. Osteoporosis leading to crush vertebral fractures and backache, or hip fractures
3. Heart disease resulting in chest pain or heart attack
4. Dry skin causing itching or easy bruising

I do want to draw your attention to the fact that the genuine symptoms related to these menopausal hormone changes occur in a sequence of time. *So the menopause syndrome should be regarded as one occurring over a period of time.* In other words, as the effects of menopause progress, new symptoms can be added to the syndrome, while others might disappear.

PSYCHOLOGICAL – INTERNAL ENVIRONMENT

Beyond our genes, the internal environment I refer to is our personal psychological makeup. How we were raised, birth order, our life experiences, education, social status, occupation, marital status, and many other such factors determine how we behave. We are all aware, by simply watching people react to events, how some individuals may barely turn a hair while others may panic in response to exactly the same situation.

An early British researcher showed how a child raised by over concerned parents who overreacted to their child tripping over the edge of the Chinese rug would have a totally different response to pain compared to another child who, falling down the stairs, was simply advised by her parent to get up and get on with things.

This internal environment will directly affect how an individual will react to the genuine menopause-related symptoms she may experience, as well as what other non-menopause related symptoms she may develop.

There are many books on menopause, even movies, and certainly websites that make menopause seem like a horror story. Long grocery lists of all the awful things that can happen are usually presented, mostly with the ulterior motive of tempting you to buy unnecessary products, undergo hormone and other tests you don't need, or take herbs, supplements or medications you could well do without.

Fortunately, the host of other symptoms such as fatigue, dizziness, headaches, shortness of breath, loss of memory, depression, anxiety, irritability, insomnia, feeling of inadequacy, loss of ability to concentrate, and tension that are blamed on menopause are actually not related to the menopause. Certainly there is no evidence to relate them to changes in hormone profiles that have been measured in the blood.

Of course, many women will have these symptoms, and there is a possible explanation for this, even though most will be unrelated to the hormonal changes at menopause. The reason is the snowball effect. Night sweats are associated with disrupted sleep. Anyone who has worked or partied late into the night and has to rise early to get to work knows the feeling of fatigue, loss of mental concentration, and other symptoms that follow you around during the day. Well, so will VMS with disrupted sleep cause a woman to wake up fatigued, and the snowball of other symptoms can follow. Alleviation of VMS should result in the disappearance of the snowball symptoms. Where they persist, despite the VMS going away, may indicate the need to search for another cause.

Minor psychiatric symptoms usually are the result of multiple factors, which need individualized diagnosis. As mentioned earlier, the ability at a younger age to adjust to difficulties in general will positively influence one's personal reaction to events in response to aging and menopause. Attitudes toward menstruation and the role women play in certain societies are also important.

SOCIOCULTURAL - THE EXTERNAL ENVIRONMENT

It would be incorrect to view menopause on a purely biological basis. The response a woman may have to the event of menopause can be modified by many factors, not least to what I call the external environment, the sociocultural aspect.

It is inevitable that symptoms may develop in response to both the changes that occur in specific tissues and body organs, as well as from the psychological components described above. But the society in which a woman lives and moves, works, and plays is of paramount importance to the way in which she will *adjust and react* to menopause. The environment in which a woman finds herself around the time of menopause will have a considerable influence on the way she responds to any symptoms she may develop. In many instances, a mild symptom may become a moderate one, or a symptom she can live with becomes a complaint that she takes to her clinician.

In simple terms, some societies reward women for having reached menopause or the end of the fertile period, while others in effect actually punish them. Many examples come to mind. In some African tribes, women graduate after menopause from being "bearers of children and drawers of water" to achieve full tribal equality. They can sit in on the tribal council and participate in decision making, and become in effect full-fledged members of the tribal parliament. Another striking illustration of this cultural attitude is shown with women of the Rajput classes in India. They experience few symptoms and look forward to menopause because they emerge from *purdah* at the end of their childbearing years. That is, they are no longer required to wear a veil and acquire higher status because they are not "contaminated" by menstrual blood. A similar situation has been described for certain Arab women for whom the end of the fertile period brings positive changes in their lives.

What is happening is that these women may experience hot flushes that can be severe, but their attitude is "bring them on!" because their presence leads to the vision of a better life ahead.

This reminds me of personal observations in labor and delivery rooms in different parts of the world. I have been fortunate in my career to be invited to teach at hospitals and medical schools worldwide. Invariably, I was taken on a tour of their facilities. I noticed that in places like Sweden and Germany, there was a remarkable level of silence, as women bore their labor pains with grimaces but little screaming. In certain Mediterranean and African countries, I knew I was approaching the delivery room by the screaming that was reverberating down the corridors. All these women would feel similar levels of pain as the pressure increased in the uterus with contractions. Some cultures have developed a sense of silent stoicism, while others have evolved an opposite approach. Maybe the response to the same level of hot flashes also has this cultural influence.

In most Western societies, quite contrary to menopause leading to reward, the strong emphasis on the youth-oriented culture may actually punish women. Being "young and beautiful" becomes a matter of prime concern; cosmetics, mode of dress, and the correct youthful image become important. Women from such societies see nothing positive about menopause, only a reminder that they are no longer young.

Other stresses are added to the above problem around the age of menopause. The average woman at age 50 may find a change of social status, lose one or both parents, lose her children to college or marriage, and she may become a mother-in-law, a grandmother, or both. Her husband may stray, become ill, or die. Or she may never have married and had children, and now have pause for regret. These are all social components that are liable to produce psychological stresses dependent on the basic character of the woman affected.

Important alternate roles at the time of menopause have been shown to lessen symptoms at this time. For example, being a sole wage earner, having a profession, changing careers, or becoming a charity volunteer have all been proven to be of value. However, the matter is more complicated. Additional factors like general health and stability, marital relationships, specific problems of the single woman (unmarried, divorced or widowed), social status, and others are also involved.

The menopausal woman's interpretation of herself, her image of herself in her mind, is thus of importance. This is really essential to improving quality of life, and something I will return to in detail.

THE BOTTOM LINE – WHY THE RESPONSE TO MENOPAUSE IS SO DIFFERENT

All the available medical research confirms that menopause may be associated with specific symptoms. But contrary to popular opinion, the number and variety of direct, true and genuine hormone-related effects are less than generally assumed.

The following classification of perimenopausal symptoms summarizes current thought and, being practical, is easily related to a woman's understanding of what is happening and in what direction to look for help:

1. SPECIFIC: TRUE HORMONE-RELATED SYMPTOMS

EARLY   Menstrual cycle changes
               Hot flashes, perspiration, dry eye

LATER   Related to the change in the body part
               affected such as osteoporosis causing
               backache, vaginal thinning causing pain
               with intercourse

2. NON-SPECIFIC: PSYCHO-SOCIO-CULTURAL SYMPTOMS

Determined by the woman's environment and the structure of her character such as depression, headache, apprehension, or irritability.

The great news is that through recognition of the derivation or background to symptom development, a far clearer path toward dealing with these problems can be taken. There are many effective treatments. The challenge has always been to match the right treatment to the appropriate problem. Now the light has brightened at the end of the tunnel.

This clearly means that symptoms directly related to the hormonal changes are best treated by some form of hormone therapy. I will address this area of tremendous fear, confusion, and misinformation in detail in Chapter 8.

It also means that you and your clinician must be certain that your symptoms are related to menopause and not the result of some other medical problem that has arrived by coincidence at the same time. Any non-hormone-related problems must be treated with their own specific therapies.

Above all, you yourself need to be in control, and here are the steps you can take...

CHAPTER 6

THE FUN PART –

CHANGE *YOUR* MENOPAUSE

There is a better way for *you* to properly take care of *you*. Over 40 years of personal experience in the medical care of thousands of perimenopausal women turned out for me to be more than a time of medical service. I was the one being educated! It became increasingly apparent that there was no average woman and no average response to menopause. There was, however, one striking phenomenon that did become all too obvious. Motivation, drive, determination, grit, or whatever you will call it, was directly related to the quality of life women were enjoying. I discussed these mindsets with my patients, in the process learning their secret of successfully traversing menopause. What follows is their secret for success.

The lesson I had learned was clear. A positive attitude was something that could be cultivated and nurtured. Aggressive development of a positive frame of mind could lead directly to improvement in perception of life and the enjoyment of it. I have called this the *GET UP AND GO* lifestyle, and my true mission in writing this book is to both explain it and to inspire you toward determined and positive action.

The *GET UP AND GO* lifestyle has four major components:

1. Self-education - Learning the major facts about midlife and health
2. Twelve basic principles - The philosophy
3. Eight essential tools - Your armamentarium
4. Eight critical actions - The to-do list

1. SELF-EDUCATION - LEARNING THE MAJOR FACTS ABOUT MIDLIFE AND HEALTH

The preceding chapters have already helped you achieve this first component. This is about knowing the parts of your body, what hormones are, and where they are produced. It is knowing how your body may be affected by hormonal changes through the menopause transition, and what symptoms or potential diseases are truly directly related to menopause, from those that are indirectly related and are not menopause related.

2. TWELVE BASIC PRINCIPLES

These principles really provide a philosophy for life after menopause. Changing habits and personality at any time is difficult, impossible for many, but reeducating ourselves away from previous erroneous or misguided assumptions to new truths is not. So consider these twelve basic principles carefully:

1. YOU CAN LIVE LONGER AND BETTER

Overwhelming evidence proves beyond doubt that positive actions on your part in modifying patterns of behavior and practicing appropriate preventive care measures can enhance the quality and length of life.

2. MANY ILLNESSES AND DISABILITIES ARE NOT INEVITABLE

Undoubtedly, anyone may have the misfortune of suffering an unexpected disease that may alter or even shorten life. But the majority of illnesses have causes relating to personal lifestyle and habits. Simply by changing these, and taking medications when necessary, you are rewarding yourself with a healthier and longer life.

Osteoporosis, CHD, high blood pressure, obesity, even many cancers are leading examples of the major medical problems that you can exert a positive influence on by changes in your lifestyle.

3. YOU HAVE THE POWER TO BE HEALTHY AND VIBRANT

Only you can influence your future by your own actions. It is within your power to decide whether to be active or passive. The decision is yours and you have the power.

4. YOU ARE IMPORTANT, YOU ARE WANTED, AND YOU ARE NEEDED

Reflect on this principle. Many women fall into one of the worst of the midlife traps, that of questioning their own value. Putting yourself down, undermining your self-esteem, can inevitably lead to self-neglect and habits that are diametrically opposed to healthy living. Self-pity gets no one anywhere. To the contrary, it is value of self that promotes good self-care habits. If you are living with a partner, negative attitudes only pull you both down. If you are alone, you are important to yourself, and need yourself above all.

Constantly bear in mind that positive attitudes encourage positive behaviors that in turn protect you and your own considerable worth.

5. YOU HAVE MORE EXPERIENCE

Of course you are a little older, but that makes you a little wiser, and a lot more experienced. Think back to frustrations you probably suffered as a teenager or younger adult, and how much more effectively you would have dealt with problems then, if only you had the experience you have now. You would probably have been a menace!

Now draw on that experience to deal more effectively with problems and reduce stress at home, at work, and in your social life.

6. YOU OWE SOMETHING TO YOURSELF

To most women the years between age 25 and 50 are an endless dedication and devotion of effort and spirit to their families, to their work or jobs, to their parents, and often combinations of all of these. Very few of us escape personal responsibilities, or necessarily want to, given that they are what bring so many joys and, yes, sadness, to the fabric of our lives. But all too often, family members, friends, or colleagues take as their right what you have given as their privilege, your loyalty and loving care.

By the age of menopause, the children are adults and, hopefully and usually, independent, your mate invariably at the peak of a career, and perhaps even beginning to relax a little. This is now the time for you to take stock and reassess what is happening in your own life. Have you given all of yourself to everyone except yourself? What do you owe *you*?

Well, the time has come for you to put your foot down. You now owe yourself something. Please do not equate this principle with selfishness, because it definitely is not. It is consideration of self. You deserve to give yourself the time and energy that is so necessary to improve the quality of the rest of your own life.

7. YOU ARE AS OLD AS YOU ALLOW YOURSELF TO FEEL

Many clichés are true and perhaps none more so than the statement that you are only as old as you feel. Despite health problems or infirmities, some chronically ill people impress everyone around them with their joyful exuberance. Many elderly people, healthy or otherwise, are terrific fun to be with. They sense life as the glass half full. There are others, even some very young, who think, talk, and feel old – they sense life as the glass half empty. It is clear that age is not the all-important factor, but that attitude is. And being a state of mind, attitude can be influenced, changed, and enhanced. It is therefore more factual to say, "You are as old as you allow yourself to feel."

8. TIME FLIES – EACH PASSING DAY IS A ONCE-IN-A-LIFETIME OPPORTUNITY

You can take the downside and recognize that each passing day is one less left to live. Or you can take the upside. My wife constantly cajoles me that "life is not a dress rehearsal." So the fleeting passage of time should not be viewed negatively as a depressing thought. Rather, it should be taken as an encouragement, a stimulus, to make the most of your time. Do not waste it. Live every day to its fullest.

9. IF YOU HAVE MONEY, SPEND IT ON YOURSELF

Many parents feel uncomfortable when they are advised to spend time and money on themselves. Understandable when children are young, but many worry even when the children are adult that personal use of funds might be diminishing an inheritance for the children. This is really debatable. If you have reared and educated children to independence, it is time you let them rely on themselves. Any legacy from you will be a bonus. At this time of life, you need to plan for your own secure and comfortable retirement. Any cream left on the top is *your* bonus.

10. IGNORE SOCIETAL ATTITUDES THAT ARE OUTDATED

Virtually all negative attitudes within our society toward menopause are fallacies based on superstition, ignorance, and tradition. So just ignore them. In fact, discredit them by your actions and your lifestyle. Use your influence within the community to change attitudes to menopause and midlife, particularly through the media. Urge them toward a positive image of women through and beyond menopause.

11. ENJOYMENT OF LIFE IS NOT A SIN

This is the time to have fun. Enjoy yourself every chance you get. Benefits of this positive attitude are likely to manifest in your demeanor and even your appearance. Having fun is contagious, and will enhance your relationships and how others see you and respond to you.

You have the right to do whatever pleases you, provided it is within the law and does not harm anyone. There is no such thing as "why would an older woman" do this or that?

12. YOU CAN CONTROL YOUR OWN DESTINY

The actions you take, the attitude you develop, the positive behaviors you activate will in many ways determine the success or failure of your life. If you take a negative approach to midlife and menopause, then your prophecy is likely to be fulfilled. If you rather take the high road with a positive frame of mind, fill those years with positive objectives and satisfying achievements, then you will almost certainly enjoy a time of reduced stress and increased pleasure.

3. EIGHT ESSENTIAL TOOLS

While the dozen essential principles serve as the foundation for the *GET UP AND GO* lifestyle that are to be incorporated into your day-to-day living, you need to consider the tools you have at your disposal to achieve your goals. These are the instruments to be used in fulfilling your life objectives beyond menopause in the best possible way. Possibly self-evident, they are often not recognized or properly used.

1. YOU, YOURSELF

It is a little difficult to consider yourself as a tool or an instrument. But it is you. It is your own body, and you have to nurture it and use it in the best possible way. In effect, it is a way of saying that your mind must be developed to use your body as the instrument. You and your body is where this whole program is directed.

2. THE CORRECT DIET

A full, nutritious, well-balanced diet is important, and common sense tells you what is good, what is bad, and when you are eating too much. Neither being too overweight or too underweight is good for you. Avoid junk foods. If you are overweight, change your diet-style. Obesity is almost totally due to overeating, and in itself carries a multiplicity of disadvantages, both to appearance and comfort as well as to health and longevity. The same is true of being underweight, because women who are too thin reduce their prospects for a long and healthy life just as they shrink their bodies.

This is not a diet book. There are more than enough of those, but it is important that you realize that diet-style is one of the most important tools you have, and it is entirely under your control.

3. EXERCISE THAT MAKES YOU LOOK AND FEEL WONDERFUL

You need to be physically fit in order to be strong enough to be fully active, to have a healthy mind in a healthy body. The first step is to get a medical clearance from your clinician, certainly if you have not been exercising in recent years. There are many ways to exercise and to achieve physical fitness. Crucial to success is to find a program that you enjoy and that you will adhere to. Here are several possibilities:

1. *Health clubs.* Advisable if you need constant encouragement and guidance.
2. *Home physical fitness plans.* These take self-determination. Boredom is the most frequent reason for stopping. Most times this also requires a capital outlay to get some exercise equipment. This will include aerobic equipment (treadmill, stair or ski exerciser, etc.), as well as items for building muscle strength (light weights, rubber bands, sophisticated machines). Give careful thought to this, take professional advice, and don't purchase stuff you will never use.
3. *Personal trainer.* A personal trainer can be invaluable in getting you started and designing a personal directed exercise program. A good early investment, but can become expensive if you persist.
4. *Sports.* Tennis, yoga, golf, and similar sports are excellent and the social contact is an added bonus. They are not usually sufficient for complete physical fitness and should be undertaken in addition to a specific exercise program.
5. *Swimming.* This is a special sport and a few hundred yards up and down the swimming pool four or five times a week is a good way to fitness. It puts no impact on that back, or those knees and hips, and is

especially valuable for those who are already having difficulty.

6. *Walking*. Here is a free exercise that combined with some simple home muscle building exercises makes for a complete physical fitness plan. Use a pedometer, get at least 30 minutes of brisk walking five or more times a week, and you will be well on your way, literally and figuratively.

7. *Sexual intercourse*. Scientifically speaking, sexual intercourse is also a form of exercise, but a physical fitness program is still recommended, even if only to improve your sexual stamina. It is not true that sex is a common cause of death in older people, and even victims of heart disease are being encouraged to return early to a normal sex life.

4. TOTAL BODY CARE

The care you devote to your body has a direct effect on your own feelings, your self-image, and even your likeliness to succeed. You realize that how you *think* you look is going to directly affect how you *feel*. It is also likely to affect how others feel about you, and hence in your reciprocal relationships. The care you give to yourself can enhance your perception of your own self-image, something necessary to a high rating by you of yourself.

Some guidelines for total body care are:

- General body hygiene
- Oral and dental hygiene – your mouth and your teeth
- Care of the hair

- Care of the skin
- Care of the nails
- Regular medical checkups.

5. WEARING CLOTHES THAT SUIT YOU

We all have our own style of dress. The only point I would make about dress is that sometimes what we wore when we were teenagers may not be appropriate when we are older. Of course, for most things these days, dress has become less formal, and that allows considerable leeway in selecting one's own dress code.

6. A CLINICIAN WHOM YOU TRUST AND RESPECT

Medical advice and fact-based care is a major tool in your armamentarium. Do not expect miracles, but do not ignore the available modern medical diagnostic tools and treatments or the sound advice that a good ongoing relationship with an interested clinician can produce. Contemporary cynical attitudes have tended to diminish the image of the clinician and the positive role she can play in your life. If you need a *NAMS Certified Menopause Practitioner (NCMP)* in your area, see the *resource list* at the end of this book (Appendix B).

7. MEDICATIONS THAT WORK FOR YOU

Medications come in all shapes, sizes, and descriptions. Watching drug advertisements on television, and listening to the *FDA (Food and Drug Administration)* compulsory list of possible side effects, makes it a wonder any of us ever considers taking anything.

It is crucial to understand that in fact anything you take out of a bottle or a sealed package for a health-improving reason is being taken as a medication. I do not care how the food and health industry tries to describe it, or what tricks are used to get around and avoid the rules proscribed by the FDA, they are medications. So whether they are supplements like calcium or vitamin D, or a so-called *CAM (complimentary and alternative medicine)* natural herbal product like gingko biloba or black cohosh, they are all being taken for a health-improving reason, and by my definition are medications. Every single one of them carries potential risk.

This is not to say that it is out of order or wrong to take some of these. But there had better be a good reason for taking a medication, and the benefit must outweigh the risk. Why else would you take it? Moreover, the quality control also has to be perfect. For that reason I recommend that you use products from reliable and ethical companies that stand by the quality of their products, and avoid the fly-by-nighters that are especially rampant on the Internet.

There are a lot of traps and hazards out there, and I will get to these in the next three chapters. Remember, you may be the guinea pig, and buyers beware!

8. HEALTHY LIFESTYLE

Beyond a healthy diet and exercise, listed above as individual tools because of their extreme importance, there are a number of other healthy-living activities that merit emphasis. These are:

- Absolutely no smoking
- Avoidance of habit-forming drugs
- Wearing seatbelts
- Moderation in alcohol consumption
- Safer sex

In an ideal world, if we could get the general population to observe the above five items and to eat healthy and exercise, over half of chronic disease and early deaths could be eliminated. Put another way, this would mean that half of the hospitals in the United States could be closed permanently and we would not miss their absence.

A healthy lifestyle should become a mantra for every one of us, and this includes men and children.

4. EIGHT CRITICAL ACTIONS – THE TO-DO LIST

I hope this is the part you have been waiting for. What actions do you take to change *your* menopause?

1. PLAN YOUR BUCKET LIST OF THE DREAMS YOU WANT TO FULFILL

If you can accept my message that menopause is a milestone and a normal event half way through life, then you should also be willing to consider this to be an opportunity to re-plan the second half of your life. What better way is there to go about this than to draw up a bucket list for what you most want to do and plan to accomplish? In the past, you will have dreamed dreams, regretted things you had not done, lost contacts with family or friends, or places you did not visit.

Menopause indicates you are entering your time, the opportunity to be what you want to be and to do what you want to do. Be critical, be fair, and above all be honest. Create a realistic list of goals and activities you truly believe you can achieve. What language did you want to learn, what country had you dreamed of visiting, what volunteer organization had captured your imagination, what opportunity had you regretted missing, what occupation had you considered attractive, what skill had you admired and believed you too could learn?

List everything you can, and add others as time goes by and new ideas crop up. Then prioritize the bucket list, placing them in the order you plan to accomplish each one. There will be a remarkable sense of self-fulfillment as you check off the ones you achieve.

2. IMAGINE YOURSELF AS YOU WOULD LIKE TO BE

Visualize the *you* that you would most like to be. Create a mind-set for a new model of yourself, the person who is going to, one by one, empty the bucket list. Consider carefully all the possible changes you can make that will bring out the best in you, make you walk tall, and light a smile on your face.

If you prefer a new image, then make it your immediate objective and go for it.

3. USE YOUR TOOLS

The tools described above are your weapons. They are what you need to use to meet your new goal of a new you and a rich life. Use every one to your advantage. Your objective is inner and outer health.

Every one of those tools is critical to your success. Use your clinician and get the necessary health checks, follow the healthy guidelines, take prescribed medications and appropriate supplements diligently, and keep at this assiduously. What may seem difficult in the beginning will become normal behavior with time. *BUT START TODAY!*

4. CONSIDER YOURSELF FIRST

Remember that you are important, you are wanted, and you are needed. Develop a positive attitude by planning positive experiences ahead. Decide to live each day to its fullest. In fact, take 10 minutes each day to plan something to enjoy tomorrow. Become motivated and enthusiastic about yourself and draw your family and your friends into these new activities. Enthusiasm is contagious. You will be amazed and continuously surprised at how your new positive attitude affects your family and your friends in a positive way.

5. WARN YOUR PARTNER

If there is someone in your life, warn him/her about what is going on lest they become confused and misinterpret your actions. More than one patient in my practice told me how, after changing their lifestyle, their husbands were convinced they were having an affair!

They may have to look to their laurels and go through the same process. Tell him/her that today is the first day of the rest of both your lives, you are both going places, and along the way are going to enjoy and savor every day and experience to the full.

6. PLAY *YOUR* ROLE

Whatever image you have decided you would prefer for yourself must become the role you are now going to play. Whether it is mature professional or senior tennis champion, the life of the party or the intellectual, a devotee of the arts or a long-distance walker, politician or animal rights volunteer, live your role to the hilt. This is not a suggestion to deceive or mislead your family or friends. The recommendation is to have a solid self-image and take every essential step toward fulfilling that image. That image has to be reasonable and attainable. So select from within your own storehouse of accomplishments the role you plan to pursue with zest and gusto.

7. GET INVOLVED

Once you have decided on the next chapter in your life, the new personal role, carefully define that role within your immediate family within your circle of close friends, within your community, and even in regard to your future in society. Be thankful for what you have, and for the spare time you have finally realized. Relish it and use it wisely.

If it is charitable work that interests you, then find a cause that truly inspires you and give of your time and yourself. If you are politically inclined, look toward local government, the school board, or seek election to Congress. If you had an earlier career interrupted by raising a family, this is the opportunity to consider refresher courses and to get right back into the thick of things. The pride in fulfillment, the independence of your own salary, the joy of being essential, all these are factors that will boost your self-image.

You prefer social activities? Learn to play bridge, join the tennis or golf club, or take up dancing or bowling. If you prefer the arts, then learn to paint, write, throw pots, make jewelry, or refinish furniture. Take lessons. Keep busy. Plan an exhibition.

And what about the garden? Develop a front yard that will be the envy of your neighbors. Grow the biggest pumpkin.

I am trying to tell you that the activity you choose is not the matter of importance. The crucial message is that you must do something. If not at this beginning of midlife, then when?

You must enjoy it. Above everything else, *GET INVOLVED*.

8. GET UP AND GO

This is my foremost wish for you. This is the time to revalue yourself. Like all things of value, your worth has appreciated with age. Reestablish old connections, make new ones, follow these principles, use your tools, and JUST DO IT!

CHAPTER 7

EFFECTIVE TREATMENTS

Here is the best single piece of advice I can give you. Whenever considering treatment for any symptom or disease, consider the possibilities in an order from least invasive or potentially harmful to most invasive. While this is so obviously sensible and logical, in the majority of instances a visit to the doctor results in a prescription for a medication. Indeed, that is what most people expect.

The correct approach to address any symptom or disease is to use the following order of attack, the Safety First Rule:

1. Try healthy living or the nonmedication route. You know what I mean – healthy diet, exercise, no smoking, no drugs, and the rest.
2. Look for nonprescription complementary and alternate medications such as herbal products and nutrients, *but only if they have been proven to be safe, effective, standardized and pure, and uncontaminated by potentially harmful ingredients.*
3. Proven-effective prescription medications, *taken according to the most current scientific recommendations.* The same rule applies here – start with the drug and dose carrying the least potential harm and only change if it does not work.

4. In certain highly specific circumstances, surgical procedures may be indicated.

The next best piece of advice I can give you is to try not to sweat the small stuff. For example, if there is bone loss and need for a pharmacologic agent, learn what options might indicate what drug is best for you, and work with your clinician in making your choice. Another example may be the interpretation of a blood test for heart attack risk. You cannot be an expert on good cholesterol and bad cholesterol and all the rest of the minutiae. What you need to know is whether the test says you are at risk or not. I am adding some detail below, but if it is in small print feel free to gloss over that item.

Following the Safety First Rule I have set above, I will now present you with the most current approach to treatment of the potential problems related to menopause that were listed in the table in Chapter 4. So, starting with the least invasive (least potential risk factors), and building up to the most invasive, here is the most appropriate approach to each of these problems.

COOLING THE HOT FLASHES

By far the most effective medication for treating VMS is of course estrogen. But symptoms are not always severe enough to justify a prescription or there is a medical reason it is not advisable, or a woman may just not be comfortable with the idea of taking hormones.

Before starting any therapy, it is essential to consider the frequency and severity of VMS and their impact on quality of life and daily living. Unless the hot flashes are bothersome, why take any treatment?

TREATMENT OPTIONS FOR VASOMOTOR SYMPTOMS

1. Try relaxation techniques – meditation, yoga, or gentle massage are examples.
2. Healthy diet, and regular aerobic and muscle strengthening exercise will improve fitness and enhance sleep.
3. If you are a smoker, stop immediately. It lowers estrogen levels and triggers flashes, and obviously that is the least of the bad news associated with this unhealthy habit.
4. There are a number of hot flash triggers that can be avoided including spicy foods, hot drinks, and caffeine.
5. Dress in layers, keep the bedroom cool, and use a fan.
6. Try a technique called *paced respiration*. As a flash starts, immediately start deep, slow, abdominal breathing.
7. There are some nonprescription therapies that work better than a placebo, but not as well as hormones, and have a role in management of mild symptoms. These include *soy isoflavones* and *flaxseed*. A more active derivative of soy isoflavones, called *equol*, is being studied and may be more effective (Chapter 9).
8. Then there is hormone therapy (HT). The risks and benefits will be discussed in detail in the next chapter. The efficacy is not disputed, and in otherwise healthy women, the risks of less than 5 years' use are really quite low.

9. Finally, particularly for women who cannot or will not take hormones, there are other prescription drug remedies that are prescribed "off-label." This means that the FDA has approved them for a different indication and not for treatment of VMS. These unfortunately are not as effective as hormones, giving about 65% relief compared to the 95% for HT.

- *Antidepressant drugs* – so called *selective serotonin reuptake inhibitors (SSRI)* and *selective serotonin norepinephrine reuptake inhibitors (SNRI)*. Well-known names include Prozac and Effexor. There is no research about the use of these drugs on a long-term basis in women who were not depressed, so I would urge caution in their use. What happens if a woman who was not depressed took these drugs and then stopped? Would she become depressed? We just do not know.

- *Anticonvulsant drugs* – *gabapentin* is the name of the one used off-label. It has side effects including sleepiness, so could help with night sweats, being best suited to women for whom sleep disruption is especially bothersome.

- *Sedatives* and *hypnotics* –include *barbiturates* and a hypnotic called *eszopiclone*, their role being best for night sweats for obvious reasons

- *Antihypertensive drugs* – *clonidine* (Catapres in the USA and Dixarit in Canada) is less effective than the newer antidepressants or gabapentin, has the advantage of coming in a patch, but does need to be used with caution because of the effect on the blood pressure.

My recommendations? For women with mild or moderate symptoms, always try the treatments in the order I have listed them. For women suffering moderate to severe VMS that are disrupting life, sleep, and the ability to function, I recommend HT. Only in exceptional circumstances do I recommend the off-label use of the other drugs. This includes women with previous breast or uterine cancer, major blood clots related to hormone use, chronic liver disease, or a strong preference not to take hormones.

REVITALIZING THE VAGINA

If only everything else in the body was so simple to treat as the vagina. Despite this good news, just too many women remain ignorant about the options and fail to address the subject with their clinicians.

Vaginal thinning or dryness may not present a problem unless there is pain with sex, or recurrent infections.

The order of treatment is:

1. *Nonmedical approaches*: Regular sex is a therapy. By promoting blood flow to the genital area, vaginal health can be enhanced. This does not necessarily need to be penetrating sex but external stimulation whether by massage, use of a vibrator, or oral sex, will all be effective. Clearly, not even a partner is necessary.
2. *Nonhormonal therapies:* There are vaginal lubricants like KY Jelly and Astroglide, and vaginal moisturizers like Replens that can be found among numerous items in the drug store that are effective

in reducing symptoms temporarily. If the moisturizers are used regularly beyond just for sexual activity, they may provide longer-term relief.

3. *Hormone therapies*: Beyond all other treatments, local application of estrogen is not only highly effective but when used intermittently in low dose, remarkably safe. The estrogen can be delivered in a cream, a ring, or a tablet. For example, a quarter of an applicator of an estrogen cream once per week can be very effective, deliver a truly low amount of hormone into the rest of the body, and is so safe it is difficult to find any adverse effects reported in the medical literature. Recently another hormone, DHEA, has been studied, but there is less evidence for the use of this approach, and no FDA-approved product available.

THE VULVA IS NOT THE VAGINA

There are many possible reasons why discomfort may develop in the vulva after menopause, and low estrogen is only one. Each has its own specific treatment. The main lesson is that if there is pain, irritation, itch, burning, redness, discharge or bleeding, or any swelling, ulcer, wart, indeed any cause for concern, then the first step is to see a gynecologist.

The most common reason for thinning of vulval skin after menopause is low estrogen. Treatment involves a low-dose application of estrogen cream to the vulva. There is another hormone that also has a role in maintaining vulval health, and that is testosterone. In fact, in my own experience, the application of intermittent low-dose testosterone ointment to the vulva has given results far better than local estrogen. This is not an approved indication by the FDA. Indeed, the FDA has not approved any testosterone product for women. So this is one of those few instances I recommend your getting a prescription for a compounded product.

Beyond the effects of low estrogen levels, the following are some of the potential causes for vulval symptoms:

- Infections, including yeast (candida) and trichomonas
- Sexually transmitted diseases, including herpes genitalis and vulval warts (condylomata acuminata)
- Trauma including sexual abuse
- Irritation from tight underwear or panty liners
- Allergic reactions to ingredients in deodorants, soaps, hygiene sprays
- Skin diseases such as lichen sclerosis or eczema
- Skin complications of general illnesses like diabetes, lupus erythematosis, or inflammatory bowel disease
- Benign tumors or cancers
- Complications of medications like aromatase inhibitors (cause thinning of the skin) or antibiotics (increase likelihood of yeast infections)
- Excessive douching
- Psychosomatic symptoms

Although this may seem a disturbingly long list, the good news is that virtually every one of these problems can be successfully treated. Just don't try and live with the problem. Seek expert care. Your complete medical history will have questions relating to all of the above possibilities, as will the physical examination. So do not be surprised if your mouth and skin are examined, or if special blood tests are necessary. In some instances, a small surgical biopsy may be required to send a sample of the vulval skin for microscopic examination.

Most times answers are easily found and successful treatment initiated. Far less often further specialist opinion may be required.

DRY EYES

We do not know why menopause appears to be associated with dry eye symptoms like scratchiness, irritation, a sensation of a foreign body in the eye, or burning and photophobia (sensitivity to light). This is not the general problem of dry mucous membranes including in places like the mouth called *Sjogrens syndrome*, and there is little evidence that HT has any value in Sjogrens, beyond some narrative reports.

The approach to treatment includes:

- First try lubricants – these come as drops, gels, or ointments – even if their effect is only temporary.
- Anti-inflammatory drugs are usually recommended as the first line of medication. An FDA approved drug is called *cyclosporine A* (Restasis).
- Other anti-inflammatory drugs include topical corticosteroids. Unfortunately prolonged use can result in cataracts or increase in pressure in the eye.

- There is some evidence that androgen (male hormone) eye drops can be effective, but there is no FDA-approved product.
- The role of estrogen drops is debatable and not recommended.

UTEROVAGINAL PROLAPSE

Most women develop minimal dropping of the uterus but have no symptoms. However, I have always been surprised how some women with almost no visible prolapse complain of a sense of dropping, and on the other hand I have had patients with a really advanced stage of prolapse who seem to be completely unaware of any problem at all.

Treatment should always start with prevention, but this requires education of women in their early childbearing years.

- Early prevention starts with pregnancy, especially during delivery, with the obstetrician doing all she can to safeguard against excessive stretching, tearing, and damaging. Tears and an episiotomy require meticulous repair.
- Other potential causes that can be addressed include avoiding excessive weight gain, treating a chronic cough (invariably meaning avoiding smoking), and keeping the bowels regular to prevent chronic constipation.
- Pelvic floor exercises, tightening and loosening the pelvic muscles can be of value. A trick I have taught my patients over the years is, every time they are driving and stop at a red light, to squeeze the vagina

97

tight as if trying to keep something in, and to hold the squeeze until the light turns green. Try it. It is not as simple as it sounds.

- After menopause there is a little evidence that local or systemic HT may be of some benefit.
- Truly symptomatic uterovaginal prolapse that does not respond to any of the above may be a good reason to consider a surgical repair. I certainly endorse this approach; only make certain that you use a good gynecologic surgeon or urogynecologist (gynecologist with special specialty training in bladder and pelvic floor). Another good tip – apply local vaginal estrogen for a few weeks before surgery. It is quite amazing how it improves the quality of the tissue and makes for a better repair.

URINARY SYMPTOMS

STRESS INCONTINENCE

Everything I describe above for uterovaginal prolapse applies to the problem of the bladder that leaks uncontrollably when you cough, run, sneeze, or have any muscular exertion.

One difference is the value of HT. Contrary to what we would have expected, there is evidence that combinations of estrogen and progestogen after menopause may actually make stress incontinence worse.

Another difference is when it comes to surgery. Here I certainly suggest you use the services of a skilled urogynecologist because diagnostic tests are necessary to confirm if and what type of surgery is necessary. Moreover, surgery for stress incontinence these days is invariably performed with an abdominal approach, except for special circumstances.

Let me emphasize that stress incontinence is not a normal part of aging, can be excessively disruptive to quality of life, and should not be neglected. Expert help is available, so make use of it.

OVERACTIVE BLADDER/URGE INCONTINENCE

OAB and urge incontinence are not the same, but close. OAB is a condition of urge to urinate that may or may not be associated with leaking, but usually involves over eight voids per day and usually at night as well *(nocturia)*. You don't need to worry too much about the difference; your concern is if you have symptoms of "need to go", frequency, or urge and then leaking before you get to the toilet. The urogynecologist will work out the cause. One thing to exclude will be recurrent bladder infections.

Nonpharmacologic strategies for avoiding recurrent infections include emptying the bladder after intercourse, wiping front to back after a bowel movement, and even trying regular intake of cranberry juice.

Strategies for dealing with overactive bladder include:

- Restrict fluids and avoid bladder irritants like caffeine drinks.
- Bladder retraining involves similar exercises as I described for stress incontinence. The pelvic muscles

must be contracted as the first symptom of urge rears its ugly head.

- There are a large number of FDA-approved medications. These include drugs with names like Ditropan, Detrol, Vesicare, and Enablex. Some come as pills, others as patches. Your clinician should be the one to decide which is best for you.
- Botulinum (Botox) injections are also sometimes of value.

Once again, my message to you is that if you have these symptoms, you should seek help and improve your quality of life.

BONE LOSS, OSTEOPOROSIS, AND FRACTURES

Osteoporosis was the first genuine long-term major disease proven to be related to menopause. Because fractures can occur suddenly and without warning, the golden rule is that every woman after menopause should be evaluated for risk factors for osteoporosis. This will include a comprehensive medical history, including use of contemporary questionnaires that help measure the level of risk of a fracture in the future (for example, FRAX, see below).

A physical examination is essential, and some special tests will be necessary.

A bone mineral density test (BMD) should be done:

- In all women older than 65
- In postmenopausal women regardless of age if other risk factors or predisposing diseases are present

- In women over 50 if they have risk factors
- All postmenopausal women who have suffered a fragility fracture (essentially any fracture that occurs from a standing height)

Ask your clinician to help you with a 10-year FRAX score. You can even go directly to the FRAX website and determine your own level of risk, but it is preferable if your clinician enters the details including the bone density result (**www.shef.ac.uk/FRAX**).

There are a number of other laboratory tests that may be needed to identify secondary causes unrelated to menopause, but your clinician should select these.

Preventive measures include all our good friends – healthy diet, exercise, no smoking, and appropriate intake of calcium and vitamin D. In truth, a healthy lifestyle that pays attention to these activities may be all that is necessary for women after menopause who are at low risk for fracture.

Once the risk becomes greater, we are fortunate that a large number of effective therapies have been developed over the last 20 years, and we actually have quite a body of information about them.

Anti-osteoporosis drugs are strongly recommended for the following women:

- Any previous vertebral or hip osteoporotic fracture
- Low BMD values diagnostic for osteoporosis
- FRAX and moderately low BMD scores indicating that the chance over the next 10 years of sustaining a hip

fracture is greater than 3%, or for any other major osteoporotic fracture (spine, wrist, shoulder) is greater than 20%

PHARMACOLOGIC AGENTS (DRUGS)

The medications that work for bone fall into two categories, those that prevent further bone loss (*antiresorptive agents*), and those that actually build new bone (*anabolic agents*). The clinical challenge is in selecting the correct and most appropriate drug for each individual woman based on her personal profile.

It is way beyond the purpose of this book to go into those details, but I would like to briefly describe these medications, and then outline some general principles on how I recommend they be used. That way you can feel more comfortable in discussing with your clinician what is right for you.

1. ANTIRESORPTIVE AGENTS:

These are the drugs that prevent the reabsorption of bone, hence slow bone loss.

ESTROGENS: Surprisingly, the only drugs that have been proven to be effective in reducing the risk of osteoporosis and osteoporosis-related fractures in women without preexisting bone loss are the estrogens. All other drugs have only been tested in populations that are already osteoporotic.

A disadvantage of estrogens is that when their use is discontinued, the bone reverts to its previous pattern of bone loss. Thus the protective effect of estrogen while on therapy dissipates within a year or two of stopping.

In the next chapter, I will deal with the overall risks and benefits of hormone therapy.

BISPHOSPHONATES: The first group of drugs developed specifically to slow bone loss and reduce the risk of fractures are the bisphosphonates. They have been proven to increase bone at the spine and the hip, and to reduce the risk of vertebral fractures by 40%-70% and nonvertebral fractures, including hip, by about 35%.

The different bisphosphonates (including *alendronate, ibandronate, risedronate, zoledronic acid,* and *etidronate*) are available as oral tablets, with dosing ranging from daily to weekly to monthly. There are injectable forms for monthly, 3-monthly and annual injection. The injections are becoming more popular because oral bisphosphonates, being poorly absorbed in the bowel, need to be taken on an empty stomach and after that you cannot lie down or eat for 30 minutes to 2 hours depending on the preparation.

At first considered extremely safe, bisphosphonates have now been shown to carry potential risks, rare except the bowel problems:

- Oral tablets can cause dyspepsia, inflammation of the esophagus, and stomach ulcers.
- Blood calcium levels can be lowered, so levels should be checked before starting treatment.
- A short-lived flu-like reaction can follow intravenous injections or large oral doses. This is uncommon.
- A rare jaw problem called osteonecrosis of the jaw (ONJ) can occur very rarely, usually associated with extremely high doses given for cancer-related bone diseases.
- Unusual fractures of the thigh-bone (*femur*) have also been reported. As a result, the FDA recommends that these drugs not be given for longer than 5 years, either taking a drug holiday or quitting completely.

103

One good property of bisphosphonates is that they produce a long-lasting effect. So even if stopped after 5 years of use, their beneficial effect seems to remain for several more years.

ESTROGEN AGONISTS/ANTAGONISTS (SERMS): A group of drugs that works by sometimes activating the estrogen receptors and sometimes by blocking them was developed to try and enhance the benefits and reduce the risks of estrogen. So far only one is approved for prevention and treatment of osteoporosis. *Raloxifene* (Evista) is not quite as effective on the bone as estrogen, but carries the benefit of reducing the risk of breast cancer after menopause in women with osteoporosis. Combinations of estrogen with a new drug in this family, *bazodoxifene*, is currently awaiting approval by the FDA.

CALCITONIN: This drug is available as a nasal spray or a subcutaneous injection. Although approved by the FDA for treatment of osteoporosis, its effect is quite weak, and it is not widely used in the USA.

DENOSUMAB: The newest family of drugs to be approved by the FDA is called the *rank ligand inhibitors (RANKL)*. It blocks the activity of the bone resorbing cells, and adds a little more bone than do the bisphosphonates. The largest study showed that *denosumab* (Prolia) reduced spine fractures by nearly 70% and hip fractures by 40%. As a new drug, long-term effects are still being studied.

TIBOLONE: This interesting steroidal drug demonstrates estrogen, progestogen, and androgen-like effects. In the largest study it reduced the risk of all fractures, and possibly both colon and breast cancer. Like estrogen, it increases the risk of stroke and blood clots. The FDA has not approved *Tibolone*; hence it is not available in the United States.

2. ANABOLIC AGENTS

Unfortunately this list is short. These are the drugs we really need to build significant amounts of new bone to replace what has been lost in osteoporotic women.

PARATHYROID HORMONE (PTH): This is actually a natural hormone produced by small glands adjacent to the thyroid gland. The FDA has approved PTH, called *teriparatide* (Forteo), for the treatment of individuals with osteoporosis who are at high risk of fractures. It is given as a daily injection under the skin with a tiny needle.

CALCIUM AND VITAMIN D

The NAMS expert panel on osteoporosis gives the following recommendations for calcium and Vitamin D use (Management of osteoporosis in postmenopausal women: *Menopause* 2010, volume 17, pages 25-54):

"Nutritional issues of calcium and vitamin D are very important. An adequate intake of both calcium and vitamin D is important for bone health and is recognized as an important part of any osteoporosis prescription-drug regimen. Diet should be the primary source of calcium because of the other essential nutrients found in high-calcium foods. Dairy products are the major contributors of dietary calcium, providing approximately 80% of the total calcium intake of women age 60 and older, and additionally have the advantages of a high elemental calcium content, high absorption rate, and low cost relative to total nutritional value.

Calcium supplements are recommended for those unable to consume sufficient dietary calcium; most women will need an additional 600 to 900 mg/day over their usual daily intake to reach recommended levels. Calcium supplements are available in a variety of different calcium salts, such as calcium carbonate or calcium citrate. Calcium citrate supplements are well absorbed when taken with meals or on an empty stomach; calcium carbonate is better absorbed when taken with food. In all cases, it is best to take calcium in divided doses for better absorption.

Vitamin D is actually a steroid prohormone rather than a vitamin, as it can be produced in the human body through the interaction of sunlight with the skin. Nevertheless, this nutrient is commonly characterized as a vitamin. Dietary sources of vitamin D are limited to fortified dairy products and fatty fish. Therefore, the use of a supplement containing vitamin D is the most practical means of addressing vitamin D sufficiency. Studies have found that vitamin D (600-700 IU/d) with supplemental calcium can reduce the rate of postmenopausal bone loss, especially in older women."

SO HERE ARE MY RECOMMENDATIONS

If you listen to the debate among the experts, you cannot but be surprised by the almost religious fervor they bring to their choice of drug. The truth is that one size does not fit all and, likc fashion, the time occasionally comes to swap one for another.

There is in fact a very logical approach to using drugs to reduce the risk for fractures, assuming of course that there is a justifiable reason for prescribing a pharmacologic agent in the first place, and that an individual's risks and benefits have been taken into account.

For the first 5 to 10 years after menopause, the best and most logical selection to safeguard bone is HT. After that, again depending upon individual circumstances, the hormones can be continued or discontinued. If the latter, and risk of fracture remains high, then one of the other antiresorptive drugs can be started. If a bisphosphonate is selected, it should be stopped after 5 years, and the bone density followed. Further drug therapy may be unnecessary.

The unfortunate individual with severe osteoporosis and high risk of fracture is a candidate for PTH.

Everyone should follow the general principles of healthy living, and take calcium and vitamin D supplements as indicated.

HEART AND BLOOD VESSELS

During your annual or routine medical checkup, your clinician will search for clues as to whether you are at risk for heart and blood vessel disease, or in fact whether you already have problems. Routinely this includes, beyond the history and physical examination, doing an EKG and sending a blood sample to the lab. More sophisticated tests are only necessary when the question of more advanced disease arises.

Your blood tests may indicate that you have elevated 'bad' blood fats with names like *cholesterol*, LDL (*low-density lipoproteins*), *triglycerides*, and so on. Or there may be excessively low levels of the so-called "good" lipids like HDL (*high-density lipoproteins*). The fact is that there is a veritable vegetable soup of all these types of blood components, and it can become extremely confusing when you get wrapped up in the details. (Optimal levels for women are usually given as an LDL below 100mg/dl, an HDL higher than 50, and the triglycerides below 150). Have your clinician explain your results to you. What you need to know from your clinician is simply whether your blood test results are good or whether they indicate you are at risk and need to do something.

The treatment of virtually every disease begins with prevention. In Chapter 4 I listed the alterable risk factors for heart disease as follows:

<u>Potentially Alterable Risk Factors</u>

1. Abnormal blood fat levels, particularly cholesterol
2. High blood pressure (hypertension)
3. Diabetes
4. Obesity
5. Cigarette smoking
6. Poor diet
7. Physical inactivity
8. Surgical menopause
9. Low levels of estrogen
10. Starting HT more than 10 years after menopause

As I address these items one by one, you will realize what an incredible difference you yourself can make in your ability to reduce the likelihood of suffering angina, a heart attack, a stroke, and vascular disease.

Again, at risk of cajoling you and repeating myself, **it has to be obvious that the general principal of healthy living is the first and foremost best weapon to prevent disease.** Absolute rule number one is to modify your lifestyle with attention to good nutrition (especially avoiding the trans fats – read your food labels), maintaining a healthy body weight, a half hour of moderate to vigorous exercise every day, no smoking, moderation with alcohol, and avoidance of habit-forming drugs. This can lower your risk of heart disease by 80% and costs you nothing except strength of purpose and attention to yourself – no visits to the doctor, no drugs, no surgery, and you save on the cigarette money!

When we get to active treatments and pharmacotherapy, the devil may be in the details, so let me go though the above list of potentially alterable risk factors.

Abnormal blood fat levels, particularly cholesterol

Beyond the healthy living there are today a wide range of effective drugs to treat abnormal fat levels.

Top of the list are the drugs called *statins*. These include names like *atorvastatin* (Lipitor), *fluvastatin* (Lescol), *lovastatin* (Mevacor), *pravastatin* (Pravachol), *rosuvastatin* (Crestor), and *simvastatin* (Zocor). These are gradually becoming generic and cheaper, and if one of these drugs is indicated, your clinician and your health plan are likely to drive the selection of product. Side effects can include muscle aches, indigestion, and abdominal pain. Liver problems are rare, but your clinician must monitor therapy.

HDL, the good cholesterol, can be raised by exercise, a daily glass of red wine (this is genuine!), or vitamin B3, also called *niacin*. Niacin can also lower the triglycerides, but the dose for these effects has to be high, needs to be monitored by your clinician, and can have nasty side effects like hot flashes.

The most effective drugs for lowering triglycerides are called *fibrates*. Available as *gemfibrozil* (Lopid) and *fenofibrate* (Tricor), it is uncertain whether the fibrates actually reduce death rates even though they lower the triglycerides.

High blood pressure (hypertension)

These days your blood pressure should be measured when you start your clinical examination, and then be repeated as you are leaving. A red flag for risk of heart attack and stroke, high blood pressure (*hypertension*) affects 25% of women. While many women can treat hypertension successfully through healthy living, for others pharmacotherapy may be unavoidable.

First round drug choice are the *diuretics*. These are water-eliminating drugs, for example, *thiazides*. Unfortunately, single drugs are not dramatically effective and so your clinician may select a combination of a diuretic with another active drug. Options include *beta-blockers, angiotensin-converting enzyme inhibitors, angiotensin-receptor blockers, and calcium channel antagonists.* Again, don't get tied up with the details, but leave the choice to your clinician. Just ask what the side effects might be, and alert your clinician if they occur. It is essential that you play your role by adhering to therapy and the healthy living side, including a diet low in sodium. It is quite remarkable how few people really stick to their treatments, despite the significant health benefits they can achieve.

Diabetes

Adult-onset diabetes is the new epidemic disease. It is integrally related to overweight and obesity, and in turn with dramatically increased risk of CVD, including heart attack, stroke, and peripheral vascular disease, the leading causes of death in people with diabetes. Moreover, the poor control of blood sugar through decreased ability to produce insulin, leads to damage to small blood vessels in eyes, feet, and kidneys. In turn this increases the risk of impaired vision, gangrene of the toes, and kidney failure.

Obviously, the answer is to prevent onset of diabetes through healthy diet, weight reduction, exercise, and lowering blood pressure and abnormal cholesterol. Amazingly, an active exercise program by diabetics can lower their death rate four times more than taking statins.

The pharmacotherapy of diabetes is varied and complex, beyond the scope of this manual. Be certain to get your blood sugar level checked regularly, and if abnormal, get good medical care. This is critically important.

Obesity

Obesity and overweight are not exactly the same. Indeed, there can be overweight individuals who are fit and healthy, and thin women who are not. Things like our genes, our socio-economic status, the rate our body metabolisms function, activity, stress, and personal habits, will all impact weight gain, and whether it reaches an unhealthy status. In turn, this combination of factors determines which overweight individuals will be at increased risk of heart disease, diabetes, and some cancers.

Beyond doubt, the evidence is clear that healthy living – good eating habits, regular exercise, maintaining a healthy bodyweight – leads to good health.

The diet industry in the United States is really big business, estimated at up to $50 billion being spent per year. Much of this money is spent on fruitless efforts to either reduce weight or to maintain that weight loss.

Unfortunately, the achievement of a healthy weight is a life long exercise, needs a strong sense of purpose, and constant vigilance. The word diet should be removed from our vocabulary if it means simply a temporary way of adjusting what we eat. For most overweight people, the sad fact is that weight loss is invariably regained within 3-4 years, as one diet is forgotten and another one looked for. We need therefore to concentrate on healthy eating, to get into the habit, and to maintain the approach vigorously.

There are multiple drugs, both prescription and nonprescription, on the market, and an escalating surgical intervention industry. To deal with these fairly and adequately would require another book, and the extent of this subject exceeds my personal area of expertize. I would however like to stress a few actions that could be of value:

- Concentrate on diet-style and healthy eating, and try and make this a life-long habit.
- Exercise every day.
- Read food labels and be willing to modify your diet style. Remember that "low fat" often means "high carbs" so be alert to what you purchase.
- Substitute a cereal for a processed food or protein through an egg or tofu instead of fatty red meat.
- Educate yourself about healthy foods, and even try and do the same for your family and your community. Get schools to get junk food out of the school line
- If you are doing the right things, are fit, and your weight is stable, be happy with yourself and your appearance.

Cigarette smoking

Cigarette smoking is a curse. Of course, you already know about the increased risks of so many types of cancer, of heart disease, and chronic obstructive lung disease, to name the most frequent killers.

Did you know that smoking causes premature aging? It brings forward the age of menopause by several years, it ages your skin, accelerates the arrival of wrinkles, has an unpleasant odor, and indeed does nothing good for your health.

So just quit! Not easy? Definitely, smoking is an addiction, which is why the industry focuses on getting kids to smoke. For those truly addicted, you need to really want to stop smoking. Then seek good medical help, including the use of the new antismoking agents. When combined with a desire to stop, effective counseling, and a search for an alternate habit like chewing gum, you are likely to succeed. The health need is absolutely clear. But the choice is yours, work at it, and once you stop, do not ever take another puff. Remember, many people have to quit more than once before they are successful.

Poor diet and physical inactivity

I think I have hammered these points home. I do not want to annoy you with excessive repetition, but I do want you to concentrate on a healthy diet-style and regular exercise. Just doing it makes you feel better and proves my point.

Surgical menopause

There is considerable evidence that an early onset acute menopause brought about by surgically removing otherwise healthy ovaries, will accelerate the development of all the true menopause-related effects by precisely that number of years the ovaries are removed before the expected age of menopause at 51. So why are the ovaries removed in women undergoing hysterectomy before the onset of menopause?

The usual reason given is to prevent later development of ovarian cancer. This is a very slim risk set at somewhere between 1 in 1,000 to 1 in 3,000 hysterectomies, and fades in comparison to the fact that the majority of these women deprived of their active ovaries will develop hot flashes, early bone loss, and an increased risk of heart attack.

Even weaker reasons include a theory that ovaries when left behind might stop working earlier than the expected age of menopause, which is simply untrue for most women; or to prevent future surgery to remove ovarian cysts, which of course might never develop.

There are some good reasons for removing ovaries during gynecologic surgery, including nonfunctioning ovaries in women past menopause, if the surgery is being done for pelvic cancer, if there is a strong family history of ovarian cancer and/or breast cancer, and when it is impossible to save them because of pelvic infection or certain other pelvic diseases like endometriosis.

The compelling reasons to leave healthy ovaries intact are to prevent:

- Menopausal symptoms that follow their removal
- Changes in other body organs like skin, vagina, and breasts
- Bone loss, osteoporosis, and fractures
- Earlier onset of the risk of heart attack
- Unnecessary psychological stress

The bottom line? Discuss the fate of your ovaries with your clinician and gynecologist before agreeing to their removal, being certain that a genuine reason exists to justify this action.

MOVING ON

I have alluded to an elephant in the room a number of times as I discussed the therapies above, but given no detail. The selective use of hormone medications for prevention and treatment of disease is controversial and poorly understood by doctors, women, and the media. So that is where we need to go next...

CHAPTER 8

THE HORMONE DILEMMA

The question whether to prescribe hormones for women after menopause has been a minefield, often explosive, for generations. My patients raised questions like the following on a daily basis:

"Should I take hormones?"

"Are hormones dangerous?"

"Does estrogen cause breast cancer?"

"How do I balance the risks and the benefits?"

"Will I get a blood clot in my leg?"

"Will hormones save my brain?"

"Are you for or against hormone therapy?"

"Why do I read such contradictory things?

Clinicians have been forced to take sides as if they were Republicans or Democrats, and not clinical scientists using the latest scientific information to work out what is best for each individual woman. So what is the truth about hormones after menopause? Do we know as little as some would accuse the medical profession?

In fact, HT is probably the most investigated group of drugs as any in the history of medicine, and while we will never know everything, and the landscape continues to change, we now know more than enough to answer virtually all of the critical questions, and to provide fact-based guidance to women as they decide for themselves whether to take HT or not.

A BRIEF HISTORICAL BACKGROUND

In 1968*, at the outset of my interest in menopause, I summarized all the scientific literature into a review stating that *"most of what is published is based on emotional and philosophical premises; the 'change of life' is an emotional subject not only to women, but to men and doctors."* The purpose of the review was then listed as:

1. *"To analyze the current thoughts regarding the menopause.*
2. *To draw attention to the paucity of authoritative research and published data.*
3. *To serve as an indication for the urgent need for research, particularly into the nature of the menopause and the methods for the relief of menopausal symptoms and disorders; the process of 'aging' and, in particular, the occurrence of osteoporosis and atherosclerosis in postmenopausal women; and the metabolic and vascular changes following acute hormone withdrawal, e.g. after bilateral oophorectomy in the pre- and postmenopausal female."* *(**Utian WH**, Feminine forever? Current concepts on the menopause. A critical review. *South African Journal of Obstetrics and Gynecology Volume* 6, pages 7-10, 1968)

The conclusions of that 1968 critical review determined my future career path:

"Several questions urgently require answers:
1. *Is the climacteric a normal physiologic stage in the life of the human female, or is it a simple result of ovarian failure and estrogen deficiency?*
2. *Are the manifestations of aging directly related to diminution of circulating sex hormones?*
3. *Can the administration of exogenous estrogen or other sex hormones prevent the manifestations of aging?*
4. *Are the estrogens at present available for administration equivalent in effect to circulating endogenous estrogens?*
5. *Does long-term estrogen administration result in an increased incidence of breast or uterine carcinoma?*
6. *Do estrogens have a direct effect on the psychological state and sense of well being in the postmenopausal patient?*

To these ends the development of more precise diagnostic techniques and methods of evaluation is vital."

As my initial investigations progressed, I became quite vocal in my conclusions and recommendations. Given the major controversy that has been raging worldwide, particularly since the initial publication of the Women's Health Initiative (WHI) findings by the National Institutes of Health (NIH) in the United States in 2002, it is quite remarkable that I summarized the state of the art of postmenopausal HT as follows in another critical review of 1969*:

"The possible major disadvantages of long-term therapy on the one hand are a fear of carcinogenesis and thrombogenesis. These risks if valid are extremely rare. On the other hand, the possible advantages of long-term therapy are also as yet unproven.

Exogenous estrogens are of undoubted value in the relief of symptoms such as hot flushes, the associated bouts of perspiration, and atrophic vaginitis.

Their use in the prevention of coronary arterial disease and the problems of osteoporosis hold definite promise but the results of long-term prospective studies must be awaited before their routine use for the prevention of these disorders can be advocated. Certainly, an important contribution of the gynecologist would be a more conservative approach to the removal of normal ovaries from the pre-menopausal female. Endogenous estrogen appears to have a definitive protective effect on the human female. Where bilateral oophorectomy in the young woman is considered necessary, the long-term use of estrogens is probably justified in view of the risks of coronary arterial disease and osteoporosis.

*The prophylactic use of long-term exogenous estrogen therapy in the prevention of aging has not been established...It is therefore suggested that only specific problems be treated and that the routine use of estrogens in all women after the menopause cannot be recommended at this time." * (**Utian WH**, The pros and cons of long-term oestrogen administration to the postmenopausal female. *Medical Proceedings* Volume 15, pages 307-313, 1969).

That was 1969! Over 40 years later, with billions of dollars invested in thousands of studies, we are back to almost the same conclusion. On the way, we had highly publicized studies showing both risk and benefit. But according to the old newspaper adage, "if it bleeds it leads," only the bad news got the headlines. Women and their clinicians voted with their feet and walked away from HT, whether it was meant for them or not.

The most significant example of highlighting the bad news is exemplified with the media response to the study called the WHI, at over one billion dollars, the most expensive investigation of a drug ever undertaken by the NIH. Although never a study about menopause, its leaders chose to report it as such, and have persisted in reporting the results taking a "glass half empty approach." This study, conducted in older women primarily to test whether HT prevented heart attacks, has nonetheless taught us a tremendous amount about the pros and cons of administering certain hormones at fixed doses to women, most of whom were well past the menopause.

The explosion of negative reporting around the world on TV, in newspapers, and in magazines, also had one great beneficial effect. Healthcare providers were forced to go back to the medical literature, do new research, and come up with science and fact-based recommendations for the use of these hormones after menopause. NAMS was the first and foremost of the national scientific organizations to tackle this problem. The WHI released its first report in July 2002, and as Chair of the HT Panel for NAMS, I released our first response in October 2002. Since then I have been privileged to chair the HT Panel of NAMS and issue multiple reports (references to the reports are provided in Appendix B). Moreover, I have worked with other national and international scientific organizations in creating scientific evaluations and reports.

What follows is the summation of these reports. The conclusions being presented to you in this section have thus been developed by dozens of the world's leading experts in all branches of health care, including cancer, heart disease, brain function, osteoporosis, epidemiology, and basic science, including some WHI investigators.

COMPARING RISKS AND BENEFITS

To help you understand the level of risk or benefit, I need to draw your attention to a major error made by the NIH when they analyzed the WHI results and presented their conclusions on the balance of risk and benefit.

Faced with a dilemma of how to explain the balance between risk and benefit in very simple terms to doctors and the general public, the NIH devised an artificial score called the Global Health Index. In the large WHI study in which they compared the women taking hormones against those on a placebo, they added the total number of times each of a number of diseases occurred in both groups. If there were more heart attacks in the hormone group, that numerical difference was listed as a debit for HT. If there were fewer fractured hips on HT, that number would be credited to HT.

I have termed this absolutely unbalanced approach, the *NIH Law of Equivalence*. In other words, the NIH essentially stated that one osteoporotic fracture equals one uterine cancer equals one colon cancer equals one heart attack equals one blood clot equals one breast cancer equals one stroke.........irrespective of stage of the disease, its severity, impact on health-related quality of life, or anything else. This is patently absurd. Can you really compare someone suffering a stroke to someone having a blood clot? Or can you compare a woman fracturing her hip to another who gets an early stage breast cancer?

When they balanced the numbers in the 2 columns, the debit side was higher, and so the NIH called a press conference and shouted fire in a crowded theater. The rest is history.

To truly appreciate whether HT will be of benefit to you or carry an unacceptable risk, you need to know exactly what the level of risk or benefit is for each condition.

THE BASIC PHILOSOPHY – *THE MINIMAX CONCEPT*

Consciously or unconsciously, we all behave the same way. We make decisions constantly, weighing the risks and benefits of our actions. We may fear terrorists, but we get on an airplane. We may break a leg, but we ski downhill. We may get lung cancer, but we smoke. So if our calculations demonstrate that a given course of action entails too much risk for our peace of mind, we don't move ahead with it. If the risks seem minimal, or worth the projected gains, we proceed. Thus we are attempting to maximize the benefits and minimize the risks.

Balance after all is an important ingredient in a good life. Balancing the risks against the benefits is how you decide whether to take hormones or not. This means you need to know what the potential benefits and risks are, how frequently they might occur, and whether you personally have a higher likelihood of experiencing the risks and benefits. The answer to the first two of these issues follows. Only you working with your own clinician can provide your personal assessment which will allow you to make a decision.

That decision should be reached using my *minimax concept: Maximize your potential benefits, and reduce your likely risk.*

As you consider your personal health profile, symptoms you may be suffering, diseases you might be at higher risk of acquiring, or medical problems you already have, the following is the list of possible benefits and risks that hormone therapies may be able to offer you:

POTENTIAL BENEFITS OF HT

- Virtually eliminate hot flashes and night sweats
- Enhance health-related quality of life
  - Mood elevating effect
  - Improved sleep
  - Possible enhanced short-term memory
- Prevent osteoporosis and reduce fractures
- Reduce risk of heart attack
- Reduce risk of colon cancer
- Reduced likelihood of type 2 diabetes
- Enhance sexuality
  - Enhanced sensation
  - Restoration of healthy vaginal lining
  - Improved pelvic floor muscles
- Slower overall body deterioration
  - Smoother skin
  - Improved muscle tone
  - Possibly better joints
  - Reduced urinary urgency
- Increased longevity

This all sounds pretty good, and can be placed on the plus side of your scale. Let us look at some of the above in greater detail:

HOT FLASHES, MOOD, MEMORY, AND QUALITY OF LIFE

There is no debate that HT is the most effective treatment for hot flashes, night sweats, and perspiration. On a scale of 1 to 10, it scores a 9.5. In turn, less night sweats and improved sleep lead to greater vigor and sense of well-being during the day, and even a sense of improvement in memory. The latter has not translated into prevention of Alzheimer's disease. Estrogens enhance sense of well being, in essence improving a "blue mood." Estrogens are not antidepressants and should not be used as such.

IMPROVEMENT IN VAGINAL HEALTH

Estrogen is the most effective treatment for moderate to severe symptoms of vaginal and vulvar atrophy, including vaginal dryness, painful intercourse, and recurrent vaginal inflammation. There are virtually no side effects with local therapy.

SEXUAL FUNCTION

Restoration of vaginal health, increased lubrication, increased blood flow, and enhanced sensation all contribute to better sex and eliminating pain and discomfort.

URINARY HEALTH

Local estrogen therapy (ET) may benefit some women with urge incontinence who have vaginal atrophy, and may reduce the risk of recurrent urinary tract infection.

REDUCED RISK OF BONE FRACTURES

Hormones are effective in preventing bone loss associated with the menopause and reduce the incidence of all osteoporosis-related bone fractures, including the spine and the hip, even in women not at high risk of fracture. Unfortunately these benefits are lost rapidly when HT is stopped.

At this time, I believe HT can be regarded as a first round choice for bone protection when started in women shortly after menopause. Moreover, as stated in the NAMS report, "extended use of HT is an option for women who have established reduction in bone mass, regardless of symptoms;

for prevention of further bone loss and/or reduction of osteoporotic fracture when alternate therapies are not appropriate or cause side effects; or when the benefits of extended use are expected to exceed the risks".

HEART DISEASE AND DIABETES

There is good evidence that estrogen therapy may reduce the possibility of a heart attack if started shortly after menopause and taken long term, for more than 5 years. HT also reduces the incidence of diabetes. I do emphasize that prevention of heart attack or diabetes is not justification for taking long-term HT *if that is the only reason for which it is being taken*. If there is a good indication like vasomotor symptoms, then consider the heart and diabetes sparing benefits as an excellent bonus.

COLON CANCER

There is some evidence that estrogen plus progestogen will slightly reduce the risk of colon cancer, but not for estrogen alone. The same proviso holds that this finding is not enough to justify it as the only reason to take HT.

BREAST CANCER

The WHI study, although stopped prematurely at seven years, demonstrated that if estrogen is taken without progestogen, there is no increase in breast cancer risk. Indeed, estrogen alone may actually provide a slight protective effect against breast cancer.

POTENTIAL RISKS AND DOWNSIDE OF HT

Some of the downside factors can be merely a nuisance, others quite serious, so carefully review the list:

POTENTIAL MINOR PROBLEMS

- o Uterine bleeding
- o Breast tenderness
- o Premenstrual type symptoms
- o Nausea
- o Some inconvenience and cost

POTENTIAL MAJOR PROBLEMS

- o Uterine cancer
- o Breast cancer
- o Blood clots
- o Stroke
- o Heart attack
- o Gallstones
- o Hypertension

So these get listed on the debit column. Again, let me add a little detail:

UTERINE CANCER

If estrogen is given as a single drug in a standard dose to a woman with an intact uterus, the risk of developing uterine cancer increases by 5 times after 3 years, and 10 times after 10 years. For that reason, estrogen is never prescribed alone unless a woman has had a hysterectomy. Estrogen is almost always combined in some way with a progestogen, and in this way the increased risk is completely eliminated.

BREAST CANCER

The diagnosis of breast cancer increases with combined estrogen-progestogen (EPT) use beyond 5 years. In actuality, the risk is low, amounting to 8 total breast cancers in 10,000 women using estrogen plus progestogen for 5 or more years. In calculating risk, for an individual woman, therefore, the increased risk should be recognized as less than 1 woman in a thousand women per year of use.

HT can increase the density of the breast making the reading of a mammogram more difficult. The radiologist should be aware of whether you are on treatment at the time you have the screening test.

BLOOD CLOTS (THROMBO-EMBOLISM)

There is a real increase in the risk of blood clots in the legs or pelvic veins, and pieces of clot breaking off and traveling to the lungs (*thrombo-embolism*). In real terms, this amounts to about 18 additional cases in 10,000 women using EPT, and an additional 7 cases in 10,000 women on estrogen alone. Most cases that occur do so in the first 1-2 years of therapy, and few after that. The risk increases with age, and is three times greater in obese women. It is possible that the new lower doses of hormones reduce these numbers. Transdermal hormones may also confer less increase in risk.

STROKE

The risk of stroke increases with age. Stroke is quite rare in women under age 60, and there is little evidence for an increase in risk on HT in that group. In women over age 60,

HT may increase the risk of stroke by about 8 additional strokes in 10,000 women per year.

HEART ATTACK

Timing of the onset of treatment seems to be a crucial factor in determining the risk of suffering a heart attack. Younger women who start HT close to menopause may have a protective effect. Quite the opposite happens if hormones are started more than 10 years after menopause. Then there is a slightly greater chance of actually suffering a heart attack, mostly in the first 1-2 years of treatment.

OTHER PROBLEMS:

GALLSTONES occur more frequently on estrogen therapy, especially on higher doses. Lower doses and transdermal (nonoral) therapy do not appear to increase the risk.

HYPERTENSION is an infrequent response but blood pressure does need to be checked at regular intervals.

UTERINE BLEEDING was a major nuisance when higher doses of estrogen were given and the progestogen was added for a few days a month. The current lower dose combinations of estrogen and progestogen these days are rarely associated with bleeding. When estrogen is given continuously, and the progestogen intermittently, bleeding may occur on the last couple of days of the progestogen or the week after it is stopped. This is not a cause for alarm. Heavy bleeding, or bleeding at unanticipated times should be reported to your clinician.

BREAST TENDERNESS, PREMENSTRUAL TYPE SYMPTOMS, and NAUSEA, are all really symptoms that used to occur on higher doses. The new lower doses or nonoral treatments rarely cause these bothersome symptoms. If present, the dose of treatment should be lowered, or an oral therapy should be converted to a nonoral.

SOME INCONVENIENCE AND COST is inevitable. This includes time spent at clinician visits, acquiring a habit of regularly and consistently taking a medication, repeated laboratory and special test charges, and waiting for test results. I do caution you to be alert for not being over tested. In many instances the profit to the health provider or the laboratory truly offers you little personal value. If you think you are being over tested, speak up, or vote with your feet.

TESTOSTERONE THERAPY

The role of testosterone as a treatment is far more difficult to address, simply because there has been considerably less research and so there are fewer facts to deal with. There are a few studies indicating potential benefit, and remarkably little showing any major harm. There are also no FDA-approved products for women available on the market in the United States.

POTENTIAL BENEFITS

SEXUAL DYSFUNCTION is the most investigated area. There is no relationship between sexual function and hormone levels in the blood, even with low testosterone levels. However, there are studies proving that testosterone, delivered through an oral tablet, an injection, or a skin patch, improves sexual fantasy, desire, and arousal, and increases the frequency of satisfying sexual activity.

BONE DENSITY is also maintained on testosterone.

MUSCLE MASS can improve and there can be some loss of fat mass.

POTENTIAL RISKS

MASCULIZATION/VIRILISM effects are the most frequently reported downside. These include male pattern hair growth on the face, chest, and limbs; and male pattern hair loss on the scalp. Other effects reported include an increase in aggressive behavior, weight gain, and an increase in acne. Finally, there may be an irreversible effect on the voice, with a deepening of the voice, as the high register is lost.

TESTOSTERONE PRODUCTS

There are no FDA-approved testosterone products in the United States. A testosterone skin patch developed for sexual dysfunction in the United States is available in Europe. The testosterone skin patches developed for use by men that are approved in the United States have doses that would be extremely high for women. They should not be used.

THE PRACTICALITIES OF USING HT

WHAT PRETREATMENT EVALUATION IS NECESSARY?

I address all issues of controlling the clinician visit in Chapter 11. HT should only be taken if you have a real indication, as discussed above, and all contraindications ruled out. Before initiating HT, a comprehensive history and physical examination are essential. NAMS recommends assessment of risk factors for stroke, heart disease, blood clots, osteoporosis, and breast cancer, and discussion of these results with each woman before an informed decision can be taken and before therapy is initiated.

WHEN IS THE RIGHT TIME TO START TREATMENT?

The sooner treatment is started after menopause, the better seems to be the outcome. It is logical and considered safe for women with early menopause, before age 40, who have a lower risk of breast cancer but are at increased risk for heart disease and osteoporosis, to start and take HT at least until the median age for menopause. They may also require higher doses to manage their symptoms than currently recommended for women over 50.

Women older than age 60 or more than 10 years beyond menopause who have never used HT will have an elevated risk of heart disease, stroke, blood clots, and breast cancer. HT should probably not be initiated in this population without a compelling indication, and only after appropriate counseling and attention to cardiovascular risk factors.

WHICH PRODUCT DO I USE?

There is a long list of FDA-approved estrogens and progestogens. Although they have features in common as well as some differences, most are considered as a class or group. There is no purpose in my getting you into a review of all the different trade products, your own clinician being the one to help you select the most appropriate product. For a complete list, go to the NAMS website and you will be surprised at the number. NAMS HT charts include oral, vaginal, transdermal and topical ET products, individual progestogens used for EPT, and combination estrogen-progestogen therapy products.(menopause.org/htcharts.pdf)

The different estrogens have minor differences in how they work. For example, the natural estrogen, estradiol, is chemically different to so-called *conjugated estrogens (CE),* or *conjugated equine estrogens (CEE).* Both of the latter are actually mixtures of several different molecules with estrogenic actions. The decision of what product you use usually comes down to trying one, and if it works, sticking by it. Otherwise, your clinician can always switch you to another.

WHO SHOULD USE A PROGESTOGEN AND WHY?

The primary menopause-related indication for progestogen use is to negate the increased risk of uterine cancer caused by use of systemic estrogen alone in a woman with an intact uterus. So all women with an intact uterus on ET should take a progestogen as well. A progestogen is not required when ET at the recommended low doses is administered locally for vaginal atrophy.

WHAT ABOUT REGIMEN – DO I TAKE THE PROGESTOGEN CONTINUOUSLY OR INTERMITTENTLY?

This is a difficult question to answer. Remember, the only reason for adding the progestogen is to protect the uterus.

When we first added progestogen after 1976 we gave it as 10-12 days each month. When the progestogen ended each month, invariably a period occurred, and most post menopausal women were quite distressed by this. So we came up with the idea of giving the estrogen and progestogen together in a continuous regimen. The initial high doses resulted in this causing a lot of spotting; that is intermittent bleeding. As the doses were lowered, so did this problem become less frequent.

The WHI study showed that except essentially for the uterus, the use of estrogen alone was safer than combined with progestogen. So now there is a debate as to how we can still protect the uterus, but decrease the exposure to progestogen. Some of us favor using progestogen for the first 12-14 days of every other month. Others continue to favor combining both continuously in the lowest effective dose. You will have to wait for more time and research to give us the answer to this one.

HOW IS THE BEST DOSE DECIDED ON FOR ME?

The treatment goal is always the lowest effective dose of estrogen consistent with the treatment goals, benefits, and risks for the individual woman. A correspondingly low dose of progestogen is added to counter the adverse effects of systemic estrogen on the uterus.

SHOULD MY TREATMENT BE MONITORED WITH BLOOD OR SALIVA HORMONE LEVELS?

Absolutely not. This concept is absurd and illogical. We are treating symptoms, not blood levels. If you are starting at the lowest effective dose, and only having an increase of dose if that amount has not worked after a few weeks, a blood or saliva level is pointless. Just step up the dose to the next available amount. Most clinicians and the FDA are in agreement that the concept of saliva monitoring is without scientific basis. If this sort of monitoring is recommended, hold tight to your wallet, or change clinicians.

IS THERE A BEST ROUTE OF ADMINISTRATION?

Currently, there is no clear benefit for one route or another for systemic HT. The nonoral products including the skin patches, skin creams and lotions, and intrauterine systems, offer potential advantages and disadvantages compared to oral preparations. There is some evidence to suggest the nonoral products carry less risk for blood clots, and on balance may prove the better way to go. But more research is necessary. Certainly local vaginal estrogen is the safest way to manage vaginal symptoms. In general, for the majority of women, it is a question of self-preference. It is really wonderful to have choices.

ARE COMPOUNDED BIOIDENTICAL HORMONES REALLY SAFE?

The concept of bioidentical hormones, popularized by the likes of Suzanne Somers and Oprah Winfrey, has created real confusion. While the term has been used to refer to many well-tested, regulatory (FDA) approved, brand-name HT products containing hormones chemically identical to hormones produced by women (primarily in the ovaries), such as estradiol or progesterone, in the wider medical market it has assumed a different meaning. It is most often used to prescribe custom-made HT formulations (called "bioidentical HT", or BHT) that are compounded for an individual according to a healthcare provider's prescription.

These products have not been tested for efficacy or safety by the FDA, and they are not approved by any regulatory agency. Indeed, safety information is not consistently provided to women along with their prescription, as is required by the FDA with commercially available HT products (the patient package insert). Moreover, batch standardization and purity may be uncertain (is this month's prescription identical to last month's?).

The cost of the medications could be an issue. Third party payers, your medical insurance company, view many compounded products as experimental drugs and will not cover the cost. The FDA has actually ruled that compounding pharmacies have made claims about the safety and effectiveness of BHT that is unsupported by clinical trial data and therefore considered to be false and misleading. The FDA has also stated that there is no scientific basis for using saliva testing to adjust hormone levels.

The bottom line is that for the vast majority of women, FDA-approved HT will provide appropriate "bioidentical" therapy without the risks and cost of custom preparations.

HOW LONG CAN I TAKE HT?

This is not a fully answered question in medical research. The benefits of long-term use will outweigh the risks in some women, whereas the reverse is true for others. So recommendations will be different for women having an early menopause, first users of HT, or for women who are in their 60s and have been using HT for several years.

The NAMS recommendation is that provided the lowest effective dose is used, that the woman is well aware of the potential benefits and risks, and that there is clinical supervision, extending HT use for an individual woman's treatment goals is acceptable under some circumstances, including:

- The woman for whom, in her own opinion, the benefits of menopause symptom relief outweigh risks, notably after failing an attempt to stop HT
- The woman with established reduction in bone mass for whom alternate therapies are not appropriate or cause unacceptable side effects, or the benefit-risk ratio of extended use is unknown

WHEN STOPPING, WILL SYMPTOMS COME BACK?

Unfortunately in most instances the answer is yes. If local vaginal estrogen is stopped, the vaginal lining will atrophy. Women on HT for VMS will have about a 50% chance of recurrence of hot flashes and night sweats. Bone loss will resume, and fracture risk return to original levels.

There is no proof that it makes any difference if the HT is stopped at once (cold turkey) or whether it is gradually tapered off. I have tried tapering from a higher standard dose to a lower maintenance dose and this appears to work well.

CONCLUDING THOUGHTS ON HT – IT IS YOUR DECISION

The risks and benefits are all up there for you to see. Consider them carefully. Some women, for medical reasons, cannot use estrogens. Others may remain fearful. In these instances, decide against hormones, adhere to all the principles of healthy living, and utilize the many other medications that are there for any existing problems.

HT has the advantage of addressing many existing problems in one medication, for example the woman suffering severe hot flashes who also has bone loss and vaginal atrophy. This can be a strong and compelling reason to start HT.

Whatever your individual situation, it is of crucial importance that you educate yourself about the pros and cons, and then have an informed discussion with your clinician. With all factors taken into account including appropriate screening, clinician follow-up, and special tests, the potential risks can be minimized. Moreover, taking the correct hormones in the lowest effective dose and best regimen can maximize the benefits.

In the final analysis, I think we have come full circle, reaching a point of quite remarkable consensus worldwide among medical scientists and health providers. For those symptomatic women around menopause without strict contraindications there appears to be little doubt that the potential value of HT outweighs its potential risks. It is the *minimax concept*. If you can and choose to take HT, individualization is the key to successful utilization of HT.

CHAPTER 9

ALTERNATIVE/ NONPRESCRIPTION THERAPIES

Not so long ago, this chapter would not even have been written. Certainly, the traditional medical establishment has been loathe to get into the subject of complementary and alternative medicine (CAM), including the use of herbal products, nutrients, vitamins, and a gamut of other methods to alleviate symptoms or slow the progress of established diseases. Rather, largely through a grassroots groundswell of public opinion, attention has been drawn to this area. So great has been the interest that the NIH established their newest Institute, the National Center for Complementary and Alternative Medicine (NCCAM) to bring scientific scrutiny to the field, and help sort out what really works. Its mission is to provide the public with reliable information about the safety and effectiveness of CAM practices, hence to shield the public from potentially dangerous or unproven remedies.

WHAT IS CAM?

It is truly difficult to define CAM. The field is very broad and constantly changing. First we need some definitions:

CONVENTIONAL MEDICINE (also called *WESTERN OR ALLOPATHIC MEDICINE*) is medicine as practiced by holders of MD (medical doctor) and DO (doctor of osteopathic medicine) degrees and by allied health professionals, such as physical therapists, psychologists, and registered nurses. The boundaries between CAM and conventional medicine are not absolute, and specific CAM practices may, over time, become widely accepted.

ALTERNATIVE MEDICINE refers to the use of CAM **in place of** conventional medicine.

INTEGRATIVE MEDICINE (also called *INTEGRATED MEDICINE*) refers to a practice that combines both conventional and CAM treatments for which there is evidence of safety and effectiveness.

TRADITIONAL MEDICINE (also called *NATURAL MEDICINE)* refers to the indigenous types of treatments that have been used for centuries within different cultures.

HOLISTIC MEDICINE is a term used to indicate concern for the whole person, including not only the physical, but also the emotional, mental, and spiritual aspects. Ideally all medicine should be practiced in a holistic fashion.

COMPLEMENTARY MEDICINE refers to use of CAM **together with** conventional medicine, such as using acupuncture in addition to usual care to help lessen pain. Most use of CAM by Americans is complementary and self prescribed.

NCCAM defines CAM as a group of diverse medical and health care systems, practices, and products that are not generally considered part of conventional medicine.

WHO USES CAM?

A 2007 National Health Interview Survey showed that nearly 40% of Americans use some form of CAM. It is now a multibillion-dollar industry. Indeed, a survey of Canadians showed that 70% used natural approaches, including vitamin, mineral, herbal, and homeopathic products in addition to their use of traditional medicine.

WHY IS CAM USED?

The complex world of conventional medicine has disappointed, confused, and even harmed many people. In desperation they have looked for other approaches to receiving relief from bothersome symptoms or advancing disease. For others, one or other of the CAM approaches has more closely mirrored their own beliefs, values, and personal orientations towards health and disease. Many have succumbed to aggressive marketing through glossy magazine ads, TV commercials, and unscrupulous websites.

IS THERE A DOWNSIDE TO USING CAM?

There is a general belief that CAM therapies are natural and are therefore quite safe. It is of course quite unrealistic to believe that any one treatment can be completely safe, providing benefit without any potential for side effects or complications.

THE NCCAM WARNING ABOUT SAFETY AND EFFECTIVENESS

NCCAM is deeply concerned about safety and effectiveness, and places the following warning on its website:

Rigorous, well-designed clinical trials for many CAM therapies are often lacking; therefore, the safety and effectiveness of many CAM therapies are uncertain. NCCAM is sponsoring research designed to fill this knowledge gap by building a scientific evidence base about CAM therapies—whether they are safe; and whether they work for the conditions for which people use them and, if so, how they work.

As with any medical treatment, there can be risks with CAM therapies. These general precautions can help to minimize risks:

- *Select CAM practitioners with care. Find out about the practitioner's training and experience*

- *Be aware that some dietary supplements may interact with medications or other supplements, may have side effects of their own, or may contain potentially harmful ingredients not listed on the label*

- *Tell all your health care providers about any complementary and alternative practices you use. Give them a full picture of what you do to manage your health. This will help ensure coordinated and safe care*

http://nccam.nih.gov/health/whatiscam/

A BIRD'S EYE VIEW OF THE TYPES OF CAM, PROVEN EFFICACY, AND ROLE IN YOUR TOTAL HEALTH CARE

CAM practices are often grouped into broad categories, such as natural products, mind-body medicine and manipulative and body-based practices. Although these categories are not formally defined, they are useful for discussing CAM practices. Some CAM practices may fit into more than one category. NCCAM lists CAM therapies under specific headings. I will briefly define them, and summarize their risks and benefits:

1. Biologically-based treatment (natural products)
2. Alternative or whole medical systems
3. Mind-body medicine
4. Manipulative and body-based methods
5. Energy medicine

I emphasize that the following is a brief summary of known benefits and risks. For many of these products and practices there is extremely little good scientific information. For updates or reliable detailed information go to the NCCAM website as a trustworthy source.

1. NATURAL PRODUCTS (BIOLOGICALLY BASED TREATMENTS)

This area of CAM includes use of a variety of herbal medicines (also known as *botanicals*), vitamins, minerals, and other "natural products." Many are sold over the counter as *dietary supplements*. (Some uses of dietary supplements—e.g., taking a multivitamin to meet minimum daily nutritional requirements or taking calcium to promote bone health—are not thought of as CAM.)

CAM "natural products" also include *probiotics*—live microorganisms (usually bacteria) that are similar to microorganisms normally found in the human digestive tract and that may have beneficial effects. Probiotics are available in foods (e.g., yogurts) or as dietary supplements. They are not the same thing as *prebiotics*—nondigestible food ingredients that selectively stimulate the growth and/or activity of microorganisms already present in the body.

ISOFLAVONES

The most studied of the botanicals for menopause-related conditions are *isoflavones*, sometime called *phytoestrogens*. They are plant-derived compounds with estrogen-like biologic activity and a chemical structure similar to that of the female ovary natural estrogen, *estradiol*.

The isoflavones include the biochemicals *genistein, daidzein, glycitein, biochanin A,* and *formononetin*. Genistein and daidzein are found in high amounts in soybeans and soy products as well as in red clover, kudzu, and groundnut.

The relative amounts of these isoflavones vary depending on the type of red clover or portion of the soybean from which the material is obtained. The relative amounts of the different isoflavones, each alone or as mixtures, are now thought to be determinants of how well they may work. Moreover, about 30% of North American women have the ability to convert daidzein to another substance called *equol*. By far the most exciting research opportunities in the area of soy isoflavone and menopausal health concern the potential benefits of equol and the unanswered issue of whether equol is merely a marker for some beneficial effect of gut bacteria on steroid metabolism. More research is needed that compares equol producers with equol non-producers.

I am fortunate to have recently co-chaired a meeting of world experts on isoflavones to translate what is known in science about these substances to what is relevant for women in clinical practice. The following is the most up to date summary of what these experts concluded.

(Clarkson TB, Utian WH, et al, for the NAMS Isoflavone Translational Symposium Panel. The role of soy isoflavones in menopausal health: report of The North American Menopause Society/Wulf H. Utian Translational Science Symposium. *MENOPAUSE* 2011, Volume 18, pages 732 - 753)

Recommendations for hot flashes

- In postmenopausal women with distressing hot flashes, initial treatment with isoflavones is reasonable
- The starting isoflavone dose should be 50 mg/day or higher, and therapy should be given for at least 12 weeks. Studies of women who do not benefit from soy isoflavones should be undertaken to monitor longer-term beneficial or possible adverse effects
- If a woman responds to isoflavone supplementation, treatment can continue with monitoring for side effects; if a woman does not respond after 12 weeks, other treatment options should be discussed
- A supplement containing natural S(-)-equol may be effective for some women who do not have the capacity to produce equol

Vaginal dryness

The experts concluded that a soy-rich diet did not relieve urogenital symptoms, or improve vaginal health.

Effects on breast and uterus

- Soy foods, in populations that typically consume them, appear to be breast cancer protective. Therefore, moderate lifelong dietary soy consumption is recommended as part of a healthy lifestyle; the best evidence indicates that there is no adverse effect of this dietary pattern, and potential for prevention of breast and endometrial cancer
- Dietary soy and isolated isoflavones should not be considered equivalent

Effects on bone

Despite the theoretical considerations suggesting that isoflavones might have efficacy on bone in human studies, the long-term studies are mainly negative, especially in view of the well-known beneficial effects of low-dose estrogen on bone. Because there is currently no compelling evidence for the beneficial effect of soy isoflavones on bone density in postmenopausal women, more human studies on bone density need to be conducted on women who are able to produce equol, soy products with a higher genistein content, and on higher doses of other isoflavones.

Effects on the cardiovascular system

The overall conclusion was that any cardiovascular benefit from soy protein or isoflavone supplements would be "minimal at best." Healthcare professionals should not rush to judge whether soy has cardiovascular benefits based solely on the effects on standard lipids. The clinical picture is still evolving. Plasma lipid concentrations are but one surrogate marker for atherosclerosis progression and the development of CHD. Independent of the effect of soy and soy isoflavones on CVD, replacement of some dietary animal protein with soy protein should improve cardiovascular health. But, more research is needed.

Effects on memory

Clinical trial literature of the effects of soy and soy isoflavones on memory supports a possible "critical window" hypothesis similar to that of estrogen therapy wherein younger postmenopausal women (less than age 65) derive more benefit from isoflavone therapy. Larger studies are needed for more definitive support, particularly in younger postmenopausal women.

Adverse effects

Mild adverse events with isoflavone use have mainly related to gastrointestinal tolerability or taste issues. More research is necessary to conclusively evaluate safety issues of soy supplementation. Note that safety cannot be discerned for breast cancer survivors as to whether recurrence or new tumor formation may be triggered.

Conclusion on isoflavones

There is justification in using some of these products (for example s-equol or red clover isoflavone) as a first round treatment for mild/ moderate vasomotor symptoms. If they do not work then HT is the next logical step.

Above all, I caution you to purchase a product from a known and reliable manufacturer. It is not the attractiveness of the label on the bottle that should be on your mind, but the quality and purity of what is inside the bottle that is critical.

HERBAL THERAPIES

In relation to menopause, the only use for herbal products has been to treat hot flashes. They have not been considered for prevention or treatment of diseases like osteoporosis. Compared to the isoflavones, most have been subjected to very little scientific scrutiny. This is worrisome because most women and some clinicians believe that herbal therapies are safer than prescription drugs, being "natural."

The U.S. government, prompted by a Senator from a major herbal product producing state, opened the door to reduced regulation through the Dietary Supplement and Regulation Act of 1994. A new dietary supplement category including herbs, enzymes, amino acids, organ tissues, vitamins and minerals, essentially reduced the ability of the FDA to satisfactorily police this industry. The outcome has been a multibillion-dollar industry and little monitoring of claims, justifiable or false. The public has become the victim, with little guidance on what to believe.

The NIH has attempted to fill the gap by publishing reliable data. I would recommend that before you consider one of these supplements you review the information relating to that product on the website of the Office of Dietary Supplements of the NIH at:
http://www.ods.od.nih.gov/Health_information/IBIDS.aspx

Adverse events and potential problems

- The content and strength of herbal therapies in supplements may vary according to the production process.
- Do not assume that all herbal treatments labeled as containing a certain substance, for example gingko biloba, are the same. Try and find a product standardized to the same ingredients used in clinical trials.
- Herbal therapies can interact with prescription drugs, either increasing or decreasing their activity; or the

interaction can produce an entirely new effect. For example, St. John's Wort can slow the breakdown of medications, increasing or prolonging their activity. Another example is diuretic or water-losing herbs that can result in a drug like lithium for bipolar disorder increasing in the blood.

- Herbs can interfere with the absorption of prescription drugs you are taking.
- Patients who are taking blood-thinning drugs (anticoagulants) or antiplatelet agents, sometimes will experience excessive bleeding if they also take substances like vitamin E, fish oil, dong quai, St. John's Wort, garlic ginger, gingko biloba, ginseng, and evening primrose oil.
- Bleeding can increase in women suffering from abnormal uterine bleeding. If you are on a supplement and have this problem, remember to tell your clinician what you are taking.
- Because of bleeding risks, all herbal products should be discontinued at least 2 weeks before any surgery.
- Many herbs reduce blood sugar. Women taking diabetic medications, tablets and insulin, should monitor their blood glucose levels more frequently when they start any taking herbal products.

Considering all these potential problems, it is surprising how many of these products are actually consumed. The following information on the few herbs that are more frequently used by perimenopausal women are listed in alphabetical order, not their value or popularity ranking:

Black cohosh has the longest history and biggest market as an herb for treating menopause symptoms. In trials comparing a dose of 20-80 mg of black cohosh active ingredient with placebo the results are inconclusive. If placebo gets a score of 3-5 out of 10, black cohosh generally in trials scores 4-6. Thus it is less effective than the soy or red clover isoflavones, and much less effective than estrogen.

Side effects with standard doses are relatively few, but include nausea, vomiting, dizziness, and frontal headache. No vaginal bleeding has been reported. Unfortunately, there have been reports of liver failure with black cohosh. Although a rare problem, some health agencies around the world have mandated that warning labels be placed on packages of black cohosh.

Cranberry juice has some value in reducing urinary tract infections. It appears to work by preventing bacteria from sticking to the lining of the bladder. No side effects have been reported.

Dong quai has been shown to be of no value in treating menopausal symptoms. Side effects include heavy uterine bleeding and photosensitivity. It should not be used with blood-thinning drugs.

Evening primrose oil has also been shown to be ineffective for hot flashes. It can retard breakdown of drugs, particularly antipsychotics.

Gingko biloba is thought to dilate blood vessels and has been used for things like dizziness, short-term memory loss, asthma, and macular degeneration. Close scientific review concludes that gingko has no predictable and clinically significant benefit for individuals with memory loss, including Alzheimer's. Bleeding is the most serious side effect. Others include gastrointestinal distress, headache, restlessness, allergic skin reactions, and sleep disturbances.

Ginseng comes in many types, and so reports on its effect and side effects vary a lot. Although promoted for centuries as a remedy to build stamina and resistance to disease, there is no real scientific documentation to support the claims. A study on hot flashes showed no benefit. Side effects are few, including insomnia, dizziness, and breast tenderness.

Kava is used to treat hot flashes, disrupted sleep, and anxiety. Small trials have shown kava to have some benefit in reducing anxiety. Unfortunately, kava has been strongly linked to severe liver toxicity and many countries have banned its use, including Australia, Canada, Germany, and the United Kingdom. Although not banned in the United States, it is rarely sold as manufacturers fear lawsuits. I advise against the use of kava.

Licorice contains many active substances, one with a slight estrogenic effect. Most of the candy in the United States does not really contain licorice, but rather flavorings. As a herbal product it is mostly prescribed to supposedly reduce inflammation, or for antibacterial and antiviral properties. There is little evidence to support these indications. The

United States Pharmacopeia warns that excessive amounts of licorice may cause high blood pressure or low potassium. It can exacerbate kidney failure, liver disease, and congestive heart failure.

Sage has been used for hot flashes. I would advise against its use as prolonged or excessive doses can cause dizziness, kidney damage, vomiting, and convulsions.

St. John's wort is widely used and is the most popular nonprescription treatment for mild to moderate depression. The NIH is studying it for hot flashes, but the data currently supporting that indication is weak. There is evidence to support its use for mild or moderate depression. Treatment, at a usual dose of 300 mg to 600 mg, should be limited to no longer than 2 years. It must not be combined with anti-depressant prescription drugs. Side effects include photosensitivity. To avoid cataracts, wear sunglasses when going outside. It may decrease serum levels of medications like blood thinners, and digoxin.

Valerian is used to treat nervousness and insomnia. There is some evidence that at a dose of 50mg to 100mg per day for at least 5-7 days valerian may work without any major side effects.

Vitex is approved by German health authorities for premenstrual syndrome, irregular periods, and cyclic breast tenderness. Regrettably, Vitex appears to reduce libido, which explains its other name of chasteberry. Other side effects, usually mild, include headache, nausea, itchy skin and rashes.

2. ALTERNATIVE OR WHOLE MEDICAL SYSTEMS
These are complete systems of theory and practice that replace and are used instead of conventional medicine. The following are some of these:

HOMEOPATHIC MEDICINE
Homeopathy claims that "like cures like," that while large doses of a particular substance will produce the symptoms of an illness, tiny doses will be a cure. This unconventional Western system offers minute doses of specially prepared plant extracts to signal the body's own systems to cure an illness.

Homeopathic remedies to cure menopausal symptoms include venom from a South American snake, sepia derived from cuttlefish ink, and some wildflower extracts. Very small doses are given. Scientific review has not proven any of these remedies to be effective. Given the tiny doses administered, homeopathy is probably safe.

NATUROPATHIC MEDICINE
Naturopathic medicine places the emphasis of treating an illness on health restoration, rather than treating a disease. To this end they utilize many healing practices including correct nutrition, homeopathy, acupuncture, herbal medicine, spinal manipulation, physical treatments involving electric currents and magnets, light, and some drugs. They focus on an individual's emotional and physical health.

Although widely practiced, NDs (Doctors of Naturopathy) are not generally licensed to practice in the USA and most Canadian provinces. Health insurance policies, as with most CAM services, do not cover this care.

Some women use an ND as their primary care provider, and regard the allopathic doctor as a specialist referral. Many ND's work collaboratively with conventional clinicians and thereby provide the patient with comprehensive overall care.

TRADITIONAL CHINESE MEDICINE (TCM)

TCM attempts to put the body in harmony. Going back over 2,000 years, it includes acupuncture, herbal medicines, oriental massage, and other ancient techniques. The approach for menopausal symptoms is to balance body energy utilizing herbs, acupuncture, meditative exercises, massage, and diet.

I personally observed a cesarean section performed in China with acupuncture in which the patient hardly batted an eye, and felt no pain. While a lesson to me that acupuncture has some role, there is limited evidence that acupuncture relieves hot flashes.

AYURVEDA

Ayurveda, meaning the science of life, is the traditional medicine of India that strives to restore someone's innate harmony, emphasizing the interaction between body, mind, and spirit. The treatments include diet, exercise, herbs, massage, sunbathing, and breathing exercise. There is no real scientific evidence on the efficacy of this therapy on menopausal symptoms.

3. MIND-BODY MEDICINE

Mind-body practices focus on the interactions among the brain, mind, body, and behavior, with the intent to use the mind to affect physical functioning and promote health. Many CAM practices embody this concept in different ways. Examples of mind-body practices include deep-breathing exercises, guided imagery, hypnotherapy, progressive relaxation, qi gong, and tai chi. Also included are dance, music, and art therapy. There is a growing body of evidence to support the combination of mind-body medicine with conventional medicine in relieving pain and anxiety, and enhancing quality of life. Certainly, there appear to be only advantages and no health risks to these interventions.

BIOFEEDBACK is now included in this category. A variant, *paced respiration* has been successfully used to reduce the severity and frequency of hot flashes.

4. MANIPULATIVE AND BODY-BASED PRACTICES

Manipulative and body-based practices focus primarily on the structures and systems of the body, including the bones and joints, soft tissues, and circulatory systems. Two commonly used therapies fall within this category:

SPINAL MANIPULATION is performed by chiropractors and by other health care professionals such as physical therapists, osteopaths, and some conventional medical doctors. Practitioners use their hands or a device to apply a controlled force to a joint of the spine, moving it beyond its passive range of motion; the amount of force applied depends on the form of manipulation used. Spinal manipulation is among the treatment options used by people with low-back pain, a very common condition that can be difficult to treat.

MASSAGE THERAPY encompasses many different techniques. In general, therapists press, rub, and otherwise manipulate the muscles and other soft tissues of the body. People use massage for a variety of health-related purposes, including relieving pain, rehabilitating sports injuries, reducing stress, increasing relaxation, relieving anxiety and depression, and enhancing general well-being.

5. ENERGY MEDICINE

Energy medicine therapies claim to work through controlling or otherwise affecting energy fields. Given the minimal scientific substantiation I could find in the medical literature, I can only provide a little background, but no recommendation for or against their use.

BIOFIELD THERAPIES apparently are used to affect energy fields that surround and penetrate the body. There is no scientific proof that these energy fields exist. Many of these therapies include a laying of hands on the body to apparently influence the energy fields. These include *qi gong* (a part of traditional Chinese medicine), *reiki* (energy transmission to heal the spirit), and *therapeutic touch* (practitioners claiming that their own perceived healing energy can identify and correct the energy imbalances of the patient).

BIOELECTROMAGNETIC THERAPIES use magnets in unconventional ways to eliminate symptoms or to heal.

SOME FINAL COMMENTS ON CAM

So there you have, in a nutshell, a brief survey of CAM.

What do we make of all of this?

The following are just a few personal observations:

- Conventional medicine has many imperfections, many times leading to disappointment.
- Dissatisfaction with conventional medicine, or the imperfections of the clinician delivering the care, has driven many people to seek alternate answers to their medical problems.
- Many CAM procedures have been around for years, but have never been subjected to the same level of scientific scrutiny as conventional medical procedures and drugs.
- Some CAM procedures have proven themselves over time and have been incorporated into conventional medicine. For example, in treating hot flashes, it is perfectly in order to start with an isoflavone preparation. If it works, stay with it. If it does not, then consider a prescription estrogen.
- Other CAM therapies are probably ready to be fully recognized, but conventional medical practitioners are usually conservative so transference takes time.
- Some CAM therapies are downright dangerous and should be banned, but bad U.S. Government regulations limiting the power of the FDA have made

this difficult. It is time for the U.S. government Dietary Supplement and Regulation Act of 1994 to be revisited and dramatically changed.

- Some CAM therapies, while quite safe, are pure marketing scams.
- If you cannot understand the rationale of a therapy or are suspicious of the vendor, close your wallet, lock away your credit card, and move on.
- It is perfectly in order to combine a well-substantiated CAM treatment into your overall health program.
- Always share with your clinician ALL the treatments you are on, conventional and CAM. The risk of drug interactions with herbal remedies is just one example of where things can go wrong if you do not.
- Ideally all conventional medicine should be practiced in an holistic, complementary, and integrated manner.
- I believe effective contemporary health care would be better off if we avoided a lot of the debate between conventional and alternative medical practitioners. There is only good medicine, confirmed by research and practice experience, and bad medicine.

Finally, do you not think it is quite remarkable that so much in both conventional medicine and CAM revolves around the principle of HEALTHY LIVING?

CHAPTER 10

SEX

Sex does not end at menopause. Indeed, the end of the fear of pregnancy is liberating for many women.

Sex is not merely the contact of genital organs or based on the level of sex hormones in your blood. We become sexually aware shortly after birth and, just like sleeping and eating, this function remains with us virtually until we die. Throughout our lives, sexuality is a source of self-confirmation and an initiator and stimulator of communication with others. It fuels our ambition and achievement as it fosters our drive and determination.

Sexuality involves self-understanding, love, intimacy, human contact, caring, friendship and fun.

THE MYTHOLOGY OF SEXUALITY

Watch most movies, read the women's magazines, consider the sitcoms on TV, and we need little explanation for the stereotype that only the young and beautiful enjoy a good sex life. That old stereotype is completely wrong.

You do not need to be young or beautiful to have an enjoyable sex life. Neither aging nor menopause is the key influence on sexual desire or activity after menopause. It is in fact the sexual quotient at an earlier age that is most likely to predict what may happen to sex drive after menopause. People with a high sex drive at an early age are likely to have the same later. Those with low sexual interest are likely to have the same level of interest beyond menopause. Other factors include your current health, and whether you have an active sex partner or are divorced, widowed, or single, as well as socioeconomic factors, and psychological, social and employment status.

One subject of great mythology is masturbation. Women without a partner, and indeed quite a few with partners, achieve their best sexual satisfaction through masturbation. In one study, over half of women age 50 reported masturbation, and this number had only dropped to a third over age 70. It can also be a method of choice for some couples in whom disabilities impede the possibility of penetrative sex. Moreover, in instances when the desired amount of sexual activity differs for each partner, mutual masturbation can be a loving way to express sexuality.

There is just no right way or wrong way when it comes to sex.

WHAT IS NORMAL SEXUALITY AFTER MENOPAUSE?

Anything that satisfies you and harms no one else is OK.

While good health clearly helps, physical impediments may change how you go about things, but should not preclude sexual relations. Individuals with severe disabling diseases can and do remain sexual. A poignant example is in the Academy Award-winning movie *Coming Home* in which Jon

Voight plays a veteran paralyzed from the waist down. His relationship with Jane Fonda is revealing and touching.

Unlike in the past, these days sexual activity is encouraged even after events like heart attacks. Arthritis, back pain, and respiratory problems may be limitations, and for those uncertain how to proceed, sexual counseling should not be ignored.

SEX AND SEX HORMONES

I have really addressed this earlier. Loss or reduction of estrogen results in thinning of the vaginal lining and an increased risk of vaginal inflammation and infections. Thinning also increases the likelihood of painful intercourse. But loss of estrogen also decreases how sensitive the skin is to touch, and this includes the vulva and clitoris. Increase estrogen and the sensitivity increases. The more sensitive a woman is to touch, the sexier she feels, and the more likely she is to be aroused. In addition, the hormone most likely to stimulate desire and arousal is testosterone.

For the woman who wants sex, but avoids it because of vaginal discomfort, the treatment is remarkably simple – apply estrogen locally to the vagina. The woman who does not want it is less easily treated.

SEXUAL PROBLEMS AROUND MENOPAUSE

Human sexual behavior has come under the eye of medical scientists, and these days sex-related problems get diagnosed into specific categories. I know it sounds very sterile and

161

clinical, but this approach does work in addressing the problem and providing therapy:

1. LOW SEX DRIVE AND LACK OF DESIRE

Desire is complicated. If desire is absent and of no concern to an individual or couple, there are lots of other ways to be intimate and enjoy life. But the woman who is bothered and concerned by her loss of desire should express that concern to her clinician. This does not necessarily imply that there is something wrong with her body or mind. Perfect health can be associated with reduced desire. Unsatisfactory personal relationships, stress, money concerns, lack of privacy, depression, medication side effects, partner performance issues, and lack of time, are examples of impediments to desire.

Physical and hormonal changes, as previously described can also be the cause.

Do not hesitate to raise the subject with your clinician. Help can come in the form of counseling, or the selective use of hormones. Hopefully a female testosterone product will come to market, as testosterone can improve desire.

2. LACK OF AROUSAL

It is possible to want sex, that is to have desire, yet fail to get aroused when the action starts. Poor *arousal* usually can be recognized by a failure of the vagina to lubricate during foreplay. It can be related to local vaginal atrophy or to central action of some drugs like antidepressants and antihypertensives. The former is easily cured with local estrogen or the simple use of lubricants. Some drug side effects may indicate a need for a change of medication.

3. PAINFUL SEX

Painful sex is either the result of vaginal thinning, or much less frequently a complication of surgery in the vaginal area. The best treatment for both is local application of estrogen. It is almost perfect for vaginal atrophy. For the women with a postsurgical problem not responding to estrogen, a surgical consultation with a gynecologist may be necessary.

The estrogen can be delivered as a cream, a vaginal tablet or a ring. Lubricants or moisturizers available off the shelf at drug stores work temporarily, but do not get to the root of the problem. Local estrogen is safe and I encourage its use. Keep the dose low and use intermittently.

4. DECREASED FREQUENCY OF SEXUAL ACTIVITY

The majority of factors at work when you experience decreased frequency of sexual activity are not hormonal. Most are related to lifestyle, especially personal relationships. Issues including fatigue, competing activities, and tensions in the relationship for a variety of reasons, are just a few examples of problems that need to be worked out. Couples need to communicate, and if sex is important, to make as much 'bed time' as they devote to other activities. If there is a problem in communication, the expertise of a sex counselor can be of considerable value.

5. REDUCED RESPONSIVENESS

This is part of the arousal factor. Being touched may not elicit the same pleasant sensation as it did in the past. Decreased estrogen does have an impact at the level of the brain, as well as on the skin and genital organs, and HT can prompt nerve endings to recover and grow.

6. LACK OF ORGASM

Sexual satisfaction in women can be achieved without orgasm. But lack of orgasm is a source of distress for some women. Many factors, as always, are responsible for the problem, including all the foregoing items I have listed. Interestingly, orgasms may be experienced before maximum arousal, and further orgasms may occur at the peak of arousal and during its gradual resolution. Thus for many women, orgasm and arousal are not particularly distinct entities.

Treatment for lack of orgasm really requires a frank discussion with the clinician, and if the latter is not sufficiently expert or comfortable in providing help, a skilled sexual counselor is recommended. Some evidence suggests testosterone may help, but there is no FDA-approved product.

7. THE MALE PARTNER MAY BE THE PROBLEM

Earlier research showed that older men had less interest in sex than older women. This may have been due to the fact that they were less able to gain and maintain an erection. The advent of the *erectile dysfunction drugs* like Viagra,

Levitra, and Cialis may have changed that. Most older men are now able to use these drugs safely. Many older women in turn have been driven to seek medical help for one of the abovementioned problems, most notably vaginal dryness causing pain on penetration.

CONTRACEPTION DURING PERIMENOPAUSE

The inability to conceive after menopause is considered to be a major benefit to most women. But remember that the final menstrual period, the menopause, is only diagnosed after periods have been missed for 12 months. Indeed the cycle in the perimenopausal years can be quite irregular. With that comes the risk of pregnancy. I have actually had several patients over the years come into the office looking for help with menopause, only to find that they were pregnant, sometimes quite advanced.

This means that if you do not want to conceive, despite your proximity to menopause, you need contraception.

Fertility rates decrease with age, that is it becomes less likely that pregnancy will occur as one gets older. In turn, types of contraception that were less effective in younger women can be quite effective closer to menopause. A diaphragm for example is more effective in later reproductive years, as are spermicidal creams and gels. The following are satisfactory forms of contraception after age 35:

1. THE BIRTH CONTROL PILL (ORAL CONTRACEPTIVE; OC) in its latest versions is relatively safe. The lowest dose forms are recommended. Moreover, the so-called progestin-only pill becomes a real option.

165

Nevertheless, there are some precautions or reasons not to take one of these pills. Firstly, smokers should avoid the OCs. Secondly, a number of medical conditions are also contraindications. These include a history of heart disease, liver cancer or liver problems, breast cancer, diabetes, hypertension, and large uterine fibroids.

On the brighter side, there are a number of potential benefits that come with the use of the OC. These include apparently reduced incidences of uterine and ovarian cancer, pelvic inflammatory disease, anemia, and rheumatoid arthritis. Further benefits may include a reduced risk of fibrocystic and other benign breast diseases, improved regulation of the menstrual cycle and periods, relief of symptoms of PMS, and there is no increased risk of breast cancer.

2. CHEMICAL AND BARRIER METHODS such as the condom, diaphragm, and chemical spermicides are really good options. They are not fool proof, but very close to that as menopause approaches. Condoms were occasionally problematic for older men, but this is less of a problem with the increased use of erectile dysfunction medications.

3. THE INTRAUTERINE DEVICE (IUD) is an exceptionally good method for older women who have completed childbearing. It is unobtrusive, very effective, carries few side effects, and is relatively inexpensive given its length of use. Removal is quite easy. One particular benefit will come with new small devices that contain the progestogenic hormones and will be used to protect the endometrium of women taking ET.

4. STERILIZATION is the last resort because it involves a small surgical procedure and is for the most part permanent. Yet it actually is the most frequently chosen method of contraception by women over 35. There are a variety of new techniques that you can discuss with the gynecologist. The procedures are short and rarely complicated.

SEXUALLY TRANSMITTED DISEASES (STD)

Just because you are older does not mean you cannot be at risk for a sexually communicated disease. The major STDs include herpes and AIDS. Without going into the detail of the STDs, prevention is the name of the game. That is, practicing safer sex is the key element to prevention, whether it is against a nuisance problem like herpes, or a potentially lethal condition like AIDS.

Peri- and postmenopausal women have an extremely low incidence of AIDS. Those in a monogamous relationship with no outside contacts have no cause for concern. But if uncertain, or about to enter a new relationship, the small possibility of transmission always exists, and preventive safer sex practice is imperative.

For a new relationship, one way of being certain about AIDS is for both partners to take an AIDS screening test. Without AIDS testing, safer sex means using condoms during vaginal and oral sex. Open and honest discussion is essential. AIDS is no longer an unspoken subject.

LESBIANS AND MENOPAUSE

About 5% of women will have their primary emotional and sexual relationship with other women. Beyond that, lesbian (homosexual, gay) women vary in the same way in almost every other respect to the general population in terms of age at menopause, ethnic origin, education, religious persuasion, and all the other differences that make us all so interesting. Even their sexual behavior may range from abstinence/celibacy to bisexuality, or intermittent hetero- and homosexual relationships.

There is some evidence to suggest that lesbian women experience higher rates for some chronic diseases after midlife including CVD and some cancers. The attributable cause may be that this is related to relevant lifestyle risks. The latter was confirmed in the data from the various groups within the WHI demonstrating higher incidence of risk factors like smoking, obesity, and alcohol consumption. Another reason might be less frequent use of health care services, perhaps partly explained by fear of insensitivity or lack of confidentiality when lesbian women avail themselves of health care.

Inappropriate assumptions such as lesbians not having had heterosexual encounters and therefore less exposed to sexually transmitted diseases (STDs), or that they are less subject to physical sexual abuse, and therefore less susceptible to psychological trauma, account for some of the inappropriate medical management provided to these women. In fact, lesbians do develop cervical cancer, and if they do not have a pregnancy they may be at increased risk for breast cancer and ovarian cancer. Intimate partner violence does occur, albeit less frequently than in heterosexual relationships. Furthermore, antigay verbal abuse and discrimination may result in greater levels of anxiety and mood disorders.

The important lessons I have taught clinical practitioners over many years is that they must ask the correct questions at the time of medical history taking on entrance into a practice, that all appropriate screening tests must be considered and followed through, and special care needs to be taken in acquiring information and ensuring confidence when counseling lesbian menopausal women.

I also advise that their office staff must be well trained and able to obtain a detailed sexual history with a nonjudgmental attitude. The staff must be able to instill confidence and to assure confidentiality of all information obtained. An office questionnaire should include questions about sexual orientation and behavior such as "are you sexually active," "in a relationship," "partner/s male female or both," and "are there multiple partners?" Useful information would also relate to bisexual relationships. Finally sexual dysfunction is not limited to heterosexual relationships, and appropriate sexual function questions should be addressed.

Recommended screening tests obviously should include Pap smears and mammographic examinations. Screening for STDs is also important. Trichomonas vaginitis, bacterial vaginitis, herpes virus infection, and human papilloma virus (HPV) can be spread woman to woman. HIV transfer is unlikely unless there is intravenous drug abuse or bisexual contact.

All the information in this book applies equally to all women. The medical care I describe above is the least you should expect.

GOOD SEX REQUIRES GOOD COMMUNICATION

We live in better times when it comes to sex. The subject is not taboo. There is a legitimate medical specialty for sex therapy. Resolving sex-related problems demands communication at several levels, with yourself, your partner, your regular clinician, and if necessary with a skilled counselor. Failure to recognize a sex problem that is causing distress, and to make the necessary communication, can be the only reason the problem does not get resolved or at least made less distressful.

Sexual activity that provides joy and satisfaction is a key component to the achievement of a really great quality of life.

CHAPTER 11

CONTROLLING THE CLINICIAN VISIT

A medical checkup at regular intervals is an important necessity, particularly after age 40. It is mandatory for your well being after menopause. One advantage in your favor at this stage is that your newfound knowledge about menopause will help in the discussion you have with your clinician about your health and your future. The purpose of this chapter is to brief you on what to expect and what you do when you see the clinician – to make the most and extract the best value from the limited time current medical practice seems to allow.

Be certain the clinician you consult has an interest in menopause and older women's health. There is little benefit in going to an OB/GYN whose main interest is pregnancy, or an internist who is focusing on adolescent medicine, or a family doctor with expertise in infectious diseases. One excellent way of being certain that you are getting to the right place is to select a clinician with the credential *NCMP* (*NAMS Certified Menopause Practitioner*). You can search for these clinicians through the outstanding website www.menopause.org. While I refer to your clinician as a woman, of course both male and female gynecologists and clinicians are concerned people with the direct interest of their patients at heart. An honest, ongoing patient-clinician relationship is a deeply valued life experience for many women.

Different clinicians do things in different sequence. In general, the first step will be the gathering of a comprehensive medical history. This may be through a self-completed questionnaire, possibly even online before coming into the office. Be prepared to answer many questions, and then to undergo a thorough physical examination. Various tests will be recommended, including vaginal scrapings and cervical smears for hormone and cancer screening, urine and blood tests, and mammography.

The physical examination is usually the most dreaded part of the medical visit. Most women, however, are accustomed to a gynecologic pelvic examination and realize that, although sometimes marginally uncomfortable, it should not be painful. If your clinician is hurting you, tell her. That is noteworthy information for her to take into account. There is no reason for embarrassment. A pelvic examination cannot be avoided, but should not be painful.

The usual technique of the pelvic examination is as follows. The external parts are inspected first for any problem and then a warmed metal or plastic instrument called a *speculum* is gently passed into the vagina. This provides a direct view of the vagina as well as the cervix. The opportunity is used to take vaginal and cervical smears. Occasionally a specimen for a bacterial or viral culture will also be obtained.

The speculum is gently withdrawn and the bimanual (two hands) pelvic examination follows. The clinician inserts two fingers of her gloved hand into the vagina and her other hand is placed on the lower part of the abdomen. She then proceeds to feel the cervix, uterus, and both ovaries between her hands. In this way, it is possible to detect enlargement of organs, tumors or cysts of the ovary, areas of tenderness, and so forth. The whole pelvic examination rarely takes more than a few minutes. Some clinicians even augment the hand examination with a vaginal ultrasound probe. This helps better visualize the internal genitalia, especially the ovaries.

While you dress, the clinician writes notes or enters the findings into an electronic medical record and this information comprises an extremely important aspect of the consultation and will be referred to at every subsequent visit.

When you rejoin the clinician, she will expect you to raise questions and discuss any proposed tests and treatment. This is where you really need to be prepared and I give some tips below. Do not be afraid or hesitant to voice personal problems as they provide the clinician with further insight into your overall case, and her broad experience will often result in concrete recommendations and suggestions.

LIST OF IMPORTANT FACTORS IN THE FIRST EXAMINATION AND SUBSEQUENT CHECKUPS

COMPLETE MEDICAL HISTORY

Presenting history
      Reason for visit: symptoms or complaints
Family history
      Heart disease
      Cancer of the breast, uterus, ovary, cervix, lung, skin
            (melanoma), or colon

Osteoporosis and fractures
Diabetes
Thyroid problems
Personal history
Menopausal age/menstrual pattern
Particulars of pregnancies
Gynecologic operations including removal of ovaries
Vaginal bleeding
Diet/nutrition assessment
Physical activity/exercise
Tobacco, alcohol, and other drug use
Use of complementary and alternative medicine
Breasts
Heart disease
Thromboembolic episodes
Liver disease
Diabetes
Osteoporosis and fractures
Allergies and contraindications to drugs
Family relationships and personal problems
Domestic violence and abuse
Current disorders
Menopausal: VMS and palpitations
Psycho-socio-cultural: Nervousness, irritability, insomnia, and depression
Other problems: Bladder, prolapse, vaginal symptoms, aches in bones or joints
Sexual relations: Frequency, change in interest or desire, pain, satisfaction, partner problem

GENERAL PHYSICAL EXAMINATION
– Note especially:
- Blood pressure
- Height, weight, and body mass index
- Oral cavity
- Glands of neck and thyroid
- Breasts and armpits
- Condition of skin, scalp hair, face, genitalia
- Abdominal examination
- Pelvic examination

SPECIAL TESTS

Tests are done for several reasons:

1. To identify risk factors for the possibility of new disease developing in the future – these are called *screening tests*.

There are rules about deciding whether to use a screening test:

1. Does the condition carry a high enough risk of disability or death to justify screening for it?

2. Is treatment during the early asymptomatic phase of the disease effective in preventing and reducing complications and death?

3. Is the proposed screening test relatively inexpensive, safe, and acceptable to the patient?

4. Is the test really accurate enough to make the prediction correctly?

2. For diagnosing illnesses that have not yet developed any symptoms, or evaluate current symptoms.

3. To follow up preventive or curative treatments to determine whether they are working or not.

MOST FREQUENTLY RECOMMENDED TESTS

1.   CERVICAL CANCER: Periodic cervical cytology (Pap smear) according to current guidelines
2.   COLORECTAL CANCER: Screening starting at age 50 and repeated every 10 years, or more often depending on personal risk
3.   DIABETES: Fasting blood glucose level every 3 years after age 45
4.   SEXUALLY TRANSMITTED DISEASE: HIV and other testing
5.   CARDIOVASCULAR DISEASE: Lipid profile every 5 years after age 45 years
6.   BREAST CANCER: Mammography every 1-2 years after age 40 years, and every year after age 50
7.   THYROID INSUFFICIENCY: Thyroid stimulating hormone testing every 5 years after age 50 years
8.   OSTEOPOROSIS: Bone mineral density testing in high-risk groups and all women at age 65 years

A NOTE ON BREAST CANCER SCREENING

There has been widespread debate on when a mammogram should first be done, and how frequently it should be repeated. Most organizations recommend a screening mammogram at 45, and annually after 50.
The recommendations of the American College of Obstetricians and Gynecologists, published in their scientific medical journal *Obstetrics and Gynecology* in August 2011 (Practice Bulletin #22 – Breast Cancer Screening) are more aggressive:

The College now recommends that **women aged 40 years and older be offered screening mammography annually**, based on the incidence of breast cancer, the sojourn time for breast cancer growth, and the potential for reduction in breast cancer mortality. In 2010, approximately 207,090 new cases of invasive breast cancer were diagnosed, and 39,840 deaths were attributable to breast cancer. Tumors detected at an early stage that are small and confined to the breast are more likely to be successfully treated, with a 98% 5-year survival for localized disease

Sojourn time is an important emerging concept in cancer screening. Sojourn time is the interval when cancer may be detected by screening before it becomes symptomatic, and varies among cancer types, with more biologically aggressive tumors typically having shorter sojourn times. Estimates of mean sojourn time for breast cancer in women increase with age. Individuals who are likely to have types of cancer with shorter sojourn times are more likely to benefit from more frequent screening when compared with those with slow-growing tumors that have a larger preclinical window.

Most certainly, clinical breast examination should be performed every year after age 40.

COSTS OF PREVENTIVE SCREENING TESTS

Earlier in the book I alluded to the Catch-22 of covering costs of preventive screening tests. Historic new guidelines to the Affordable Care Act that will ensure women receive preventive health services at no additional cost were announced on August 1st, 2011, by the U.S. Department of Health and Human Services (HHS). Developed by the independent Institute of Medicine, the new guidelines require new health insurance plans to cover women's preventive services such as well-woman visits, domestic violence screening, and contraception, without charging a co-payment, co-insurance or a deductible.

These historic guidelines are based on science and existing literature and will help ensure women get the preventive health benefits they need. Often because of cost, Americans used preventive services at about half the recommended rate. The Affordable Care Act requires all new private health plans to cover several evidence-based preventive services like mammograms, colonoscopies, and blood pressure checks, without charging a copayment, deductible or coinsurance. The Affordable Care Act also made recommended preventive services free for people on Medicare.

Hopefully, if the law remains intact, women will have access to a full range of recommended preventive services without cost sharing, including:
- well-woman visits
- screening for gestational diabetes
- human papillomavirus (HPV) DNA testing for women 30 years and older
- sexually-transmitted infection counseling;
- human immunodeficiency virus (HIV) screening and counseling
- FDA-approved contraception methods and contraceptive counseling
- domestic violence screening and counseling

QUESTIONS TO ASK YOUR CLINICIAN

Many of your questions will have been answered in the preceding pages. To gain maximum benefit from the limited time with your clinician it is essential that you are prepared with your questions you need answered. Some questions are generic, meaning everyone should ask them. Others will be more specific to your own concerns.

Like the boy scouts, be prepared. Take your list of questions with you. As you ask your questions, make certain you keep the conversation focused, keep the clinician on track, and do not get into unnecessary conversation. Many has been the time that a patient in my office started describing problems about a friend, a cousin, or someone else, and completely forgot that the limited time she was spending with me was only about herself.

GENERAL QUESTIONS
1. Have I gone through menopause?
2. Do I have risk factors for any serious diseases?
3. Do I already have a disease in an early stage that has not yet become symptomatic?
4. Are there any other tests that I should have?
5. If you are recommending a bone density test, why?
6. How will the results of my special tests get reported to me?
7. Do you recommend any dietary supplements, vitamins, or minerals?
7. In regard to healthy living, what am I not doing right?
8. Are there any non-prescription drugs I can try first for my symptoms?
9. Am I a candidate for any drugs that might reduce the risks of disease?
8. What are the risks versus the benefits of my not taking some form of hormone therapy?
10. Who do I speak to in the office to get answers to new questions or concerns?
11. What is your plan for my future visits and screening tests?

SPECIFIC QUESTIONS
These are the questions that relate to your own personal circumstances. I can only give some broad examples. You should give this some thought before you go to the clinician, otherwise time will run out before you know it:

179

1. I had a blood clot in my leg with my first pregnancy. Does this preclude me from taking hormones?
2. I broke my collarbone in a car accident. Does this mean I have osteoporosis?
3. My Pap smears were abnormal 20 years ago. Am I at increased risk for cancer anywhere in my body?
4. Every older woman in my family has had a heart attack. Will hormones be a risk or a benefit for me?

I can go on giving dozens of examples. After all that was what I did for a living for many years! But you get the gist of what I am saying – be aware of your own health concerns and problems, and get answers to questions that concern you directly.

SUMMING UP YOUR VISIT TO YOUR CLINICIAN

The clinician is but one tool in your armamentarium towards enhancing the quality and quantity of your life. Select your clinician with care. Make the appointment, prepare your questions, be certain you get answers, and above all consider the advice you are given carefully.

It serves little purpose going through all of this if you do not plan to follow through with recommendations. Seventy five per cent of women at high risk of osteoporotic fractures stop taking their prescribed bone medicines within less than 2 years. The same can be said of blood pressure reducing drugs. Failure to stick to therapy is called poor adherence. Do not be one of the offenders. The only loser will be you.

CHAPTER 12

MEN AND MENOPAUSE –

THE ANDROPAUSE

What happens to men in middle age? While the Bible described life expectancy as "three score years and ten" and half of 70 years would have meant middle age starts at 35, modern life expectancy for men is longer. Middle age can be more accurately said to start at between 40 and 45.

So why around that age do men tend to stray, buy a red sports car, get restless at work, and throw a fit when addressed by an attractive young assistant as "sir" for the first time? I suppose this leads to the question as to whether there is a male menopause. More accurately, are there equivalent hormonal changes, and are men also subject to the psycho-socio-cultural effects of aging?

Frankly, there is just no male menopause if loss of fertility and hormones is what defines it. The term *male menopause* is also manifestly ridiculous. Men do not menstruate so how could they stop menstruating? For want of a better descriptive term of this phase in life, another word is coming into popular use – *andropause*.

Something does seem to happen to men traversing andropause. How can we explain it?

AGE-RELATED HORMONE CHANGES IN MEN

The testis is just not an ovary. While the ovary is endowed at birth with all the eggs it will ever have, and essentially runs out by menopause, the testis is like the Energizer bunny and just keeps going and going. That is why old men can still be fertile. I am sure that one day we may find a reason behind all this, but for now we can only speculate.

So while the ovary runs out of eggs and produces less and less hormones through menopause, the testis goes on producing its sperms and hormones into much older age. The production of testosterone, the key male hormone, does peak at around age 50, but a subsequent gradual reduction takes place over the subsequent 30 to 40 years. Some men do exhibit an earlier and more rapid decline in testosterone levels than others. Sperm counts will also decline in older age, but remain capable of fertilizing an egg. Obviously, there is little comparison with the abrupt changes that occur in women.

ARE THERE GENUINE SYMPTOMS RELATED TO ANDROPAUSE?

If there are, no one has really been able to prove they exist. As men age they do complain of reduced libido or sexual potency, increased fatigue, a decreasing ability to concentrate and be productive, sleep disturbances, anxiety, and depression. Some men even report hot flashes, sweating, and rapid heart beats (*palpitations*).

None of these symptoms can be related to any of the hormonal changes. Most likely they are effects of aging itself, certainly those related to sex, memory, and sleep. All these symptoms just slowly get worse with age. Watching athletes' age would seem to confirm this.

SO WHAT IS THIS PHENOMENON CALLED ANDROPAUSE?

Accepting the multiple reports of behavioral changes in some men in their middle years does call for an explanation. I personally believe this can be very easily explained.

Recall in Chapter 5 how I explained why the menopause experience was so different between women? Hormone changes in women were shown to account for remarkably few symptoms. The rest of the many symptoms so often described in magazines and talk shows were shown to be the outcome of differences in the psychological, social, and economic backgrounds of women.

We all live on the same planet. So why cannot this principle also not apply to men? Thus, because there is no male hormonal equivalent of the female menopause transition, it is not surprising that we are unable to find any symptoms in men absolutely related to their hormone levels. But it should be obvious to all that men are subject to the impact of their own psychological, social, and economic backgrounds. I would add that for many men this might even be more so than in women.

There are many circumstances to exemplify this. In the animal world the male battles to maintain dominance. Did you see *The Lion King*? In the human world, a highly successful man may feel he has peaked, worries about his future, and may need to battle to stay top of the heap. Another may feel a need for outside recognition of his powers, accomplishments, or attractiveness. Others feel the approach of older age, want another bite of the apple, and enter a phase of frantic or erratic behavior. Yet another may recognize personal failures and be looking for a way out. These situations are different for each man and are therefore more of a problem for some than for others.

Social scientists report that every man reaches a time of reflection and personal evaluation. Some handle it well; others are terrified by the experience. The former will handle things smoothly, making adjustments in a thoughtful and responsible way. The latter may become emotionally overwrought and convert that turmoil into some apparently senseless decisions. These may include reassurance by surrounding themselves with material objects to serve as an indicator of success, or a new relationship with a younger woman, or a decision to give up work and climb Mount Everest, proof of being a great male macho.

Men may also have a greater fear of death than women. Remember, men are the weaker sex and die at an earlier age than women. Consequently, at a younger age they are more likely to be losing male friends, school mates, business partners, and family, from diseases like heart attacks, diabetes, prostate cancer, and other medical problems.

Men have two other disadvantages compared to women. In many societies they are raised to hide emotion; to cry is a sign of weakness, whereas women can freely express emotion. Thus they bottle feelings up, and when at last they need to vent, the reaction can be explosive. The other disadvantage is that men and women socialize differently. Women socialize in groups, share personal problems, and laugh and cry together. Men do not. When in groups, they will speak sports, cars, and the stock exchange. Men do not generally share emotional or personal problems.

So the fallout of the psychological, social, and economic differences will vary. In some men the outcome will be productive. In others it can result in a major behavioral change, an emotional depression, and even suicide.

My conclusion is that for men, andropause is not a hormonal or physical change-related phenomenon, but a behavioral change based on a complex set of personal factors.

WHAT CAN THE PERIMENOPAUSAL WOMAN DO TO MAINTAIN A HEALTHY RELATIONSHIP?

If maintaining a long-term and solid relationship is what she wants, then there is indeed much that the perimenopausal woman can do.

In my book *THE UTIAN STRATEGY – Is this my problem or is this your problem*? I would clearly recognize the problem to be his. But as I describe management of such problems in that book, I emphasize that in family situations the best solution can be to take joint ownership. This would be one such situation.

I think the first step is to recognize a developing situation. The next is to have an open and honest discussion – communication is key to success. Explain that you are both going through a major phase of transition in life. Share aspects of the action plan, the GET UP AND GO Lifestyle, described in Chapter 6. Finally, work together, stimulate each other, be supportive at the bad times, avoid hostility, and together develop an enthusiasm for mutual growth and enjoyment of the second half of your lives.

WHAT CAN A MAN DO FOR HIMSELF?

He may need help, but *recognition* of what is going on in his life is half way to the solution. Beyond recognition there is *action*. Action is encouraged by problem recognition and awareness that there are many constructive ways to move forward into a successful, productive, and enjoyable older age.

Chapter 6 is essential reading for the man or men in your life, as much as it is for the women. But they must take the active steps; understand the principles, appreciate the tools, and take the actions.

Men are not good consumers of health care. Often they are taken, kicking and screaming against their wills, by their wives to a clinician for a health check up. But given the higher prevalence of many serious diseases in men, starting at a younger age than in women, a health check up is mandatory.

A low testosterone level may be identified in a minority of men. Here, replacement therapy with testosterone may result in improved libido, greater vigor, increased muscle mass, and reduced fat mass. There may be a small increase in the risk of prostate cancer. This is an area for discussion between the man and his clinician.

After that, all the other actions apply, namely, healthy living, a new focus of productive activity, combined outings, shared projects, and so on.

CONCLUDING THOUGHTS

There is no male menopause as a hormonal event. But men in their middle years are vulnerable to a number of emotional issues based on their psycho-socio-cultural background. Recognition of this is crucial to actively and successfully managing the second half of life.

Couples can work together in achieving these goals through direct communication and assertive actions.

I hope that one of the outcomes of this book will be to encourage such communication and recognition that aging is a natural phenomenon, and that working together you can discover things each of you can do to excite and enhance each other's life and the life you share. Instead of being reactive to each other, the key to success is to become restorative together.

CHAPTER 13

NOW IT IS YOUR TIME – GET UP AND GO!

So there you have it all in a nutshell. Menopause is not a disease. It is a phase of life. It is the milestone as you travel through one chapter of life to the next. Indeed, most women need no direct medical interventions to achieve a healthy and rewarding quality of life beyond menopause.

But it is a wonderful opportunity to take stock, to reevaluate where you are and where you want to go. It is the indicator of need for a good medical checkup, to identify health risk factors for the future, and even undiagnosed early disease. It is the signal to concentrate on healthy living and fulfilling your bucket list, your dream list of all the things you want to do and achieve in this second half of your life.

So I conclude this menopause manual by repeating the mantra I gave earlier:

1. Create your bucket list to live your dreams.
2. Use the tools identified in Chapter 6.
3. Consider yourself first.
4. Warn your partner.
5. Play *your* role.
6. Get involved.
7. Get up and GO – CHANGE *YOUR* MENOPAUSE!

And above all, keep at it.

I wish you a joyful life of good health, exuberance, and fun with family and friends.

Wulf Utian
Cleveland, Ohio, and Cape Town, South Africa

APPENDIX A

FURTHER READING

TEXTBOOK

Menopause Practice – A Clinician's Guide, 4th Edition, The North American Menopause Society, 2010.

This is the definitive textbook on the subject written for clinicians. Informed readers can search the book for greater detail about specific issues.

POSITION STATEMENTS

1.   Utian WH (Panel Chair). Estrogen and progestogen use in postmenopausal women: 2010 position statement of The North American Menopause Society. *MENOPAUSE* 2010;17:242-255.

2.   Santen RJ, Utian WH et al. Postmenopausal Hormone Therapy: An Endocrine Society Scientific Statement. *J. Clin. Endocrinol. Metab.* 2010;95, Supplement:S1-S66.

3.   Clarkson TB, Utian WH, Barnes S, et al, for the NAMS Isoflavone Translational Symposium Panel. The role of soy isoflavones in menopausal health: report of The North American Menopause Society/Wulf H. Utian Translational Science Symposium in Chicago, IL . *MENOPAUSE* 2011;18: 732-753

4.   Management of osteoporosis in postmenopausal women: 2010 position statement of the North American Menopause Society. *MENOPAUSE* 2010;17:25-54

GENERAL READING

The Hormone Decision, Tara Parker Pope, Rodale, New York, 2007. This is an in-depth look at the story behind the WHI study.

Our Bodies Ourselves Menopause, The Boston Women's Health Book Collective, Touchstone, New York, 2006. Further detail and good clinical advice, but somewhat out of date on the latest findings regarding some medications.

APPENDIX B

USEFUL AND TRUSTWORTHY RESOURCES

THE NORTH AMERICAN MENOPAUSE SOCIETY (NAMS)
P.O. Box 94527,
Cleveland,
OH 44101
Tel. 440 4427550
info@menopause.org
www.menopause.org

This is the pre-eminent non-profit multispecialty organization providing the best non-biased, non-commercial information on all aspects of menopause.

FIND A NAMS CERTIFIED MENOPAUSE PRACTITIONER
NAMS is the only organization with a certification program requiring passing a comprehensive examination that leads to the credential NCMP (NAMS Certified Menopause Practitioner). For an NCMP near you, access the NAMS website at:
http://www.menopause.org/findclinician.aspx

LIST OF AVAILABLE ESTROGEN AND PROGESTOGEN MEDICATIONS IN THE USA AND CANADA
A regularly updated list of all the drugs with both trade and generic names is provided by NAMS at:
menopause.org/htcharts.pdf

ASSESSING FRACTURE RISK
The FRAX score can be measured by entering information at this site. You will probably need assistance from your clinician. **www.shef.ac.uk/FRAX**

REPUTABLE WEBSITES

National Library of Medicine has partnered with ORWH to create the Women's Health Resources Web portal: www.womenshealthresources.nlm.nih.gov. This site gives researchers and consumers access to the latest information about significant topics in women's health from scientific journals, peer-reviewed sources, NIH Institutes and Centers, and health news sources.

North American Menopause Society - NAMS
www.menopause.org

American College of Obstetrics and Gynecology
www.acog.org

American Dietetic Association
www.eatright.org

National Association of Nurse Practitioners in Women's Health
www.npwh.org

Society for Women's Health Research
www.womenshealthresearch.org

National Osteoporosis Foundation
www.nof.org

U.S. Department of Health and Human Services
www.health.gov

The International Premature Ovarian Failure Association
www.pofsupport.org

Black Women's Health Imperative
www.blackwomenshealth.org

Canadian Women's Health Network
www.cwhn.ca

OWL: Older Women's League, The Voice of Midlife and Older Women
www.owl-national.org

National Center for Complementary and Alternative Medicine at NIH (NCCAM)
http://nccam.nih.gov/health

Food and Drug Administration (FDA)
www.fda.gov

APPENDIX C

FREQUENTLY ASKED QUESTIONS

Q.   **Can I get pregnant** as I go through the menopause?

A.   Pregnancy remains a possibility even if you miss periods by a few months. Pregnancy is unlikely after age 50 and there have been no periods for 12 months.

Q.   If I had a **hysterectomy** and my ovaries were saved, will my menopause arrive earlier?

A.   While possible for some women, most times the conserved ovaries continue to function.

Q.   What **tests and exams** will I need to monitor my health as I approach menopause?

A.   See page 175-177.

Q.   Is it in order to try a **plant estrogen like equol** before taking a prescription drug?

A.   This is a logical approach, especially if the hot flashes are mild or moderate. Be certain to look for a quality product. If after a few weeks alternate therapies are not helping, you may feel more at ease about starting an estrogen.

Q.   If I start taking **hormones, does this mean I take them forever**, and what happens when I stop?

A.   No, you will take them from one clinician checkup to the next, and decide each year whether the benefits of continuing outweigh the risks.

Q.   What is the difference of taking **hormones by mouth as compared to through the skin**?

A.   See page 135.

Q.   What are **natural or bioidentical hormones**?

A.   See page 135-6.

Q.   How will I know I am menopausal if I have had a **hysterectomy**?

A.   You may develop true menopausal symptoms, or a blood test may show your FSH level to be elevated.

Q.   What are the **risks of having a bone density test**?

A.   There is a very small radiation dose. Given the test should be done every 2 years at the most, the risk is truly small.

Q.   I went through the menopause 13 years ago. Is it **too late to start hormones**?

A.   Unfortunately the answer is most likely yes. This requires careful discussion with your clinician, and there should be an overwhelming indication to take the meds. The exception is low dose intermittent vaginal estrogen for vaginal thinning. This is safe.

Q.   I have had **breast cancer**. Can I take hormone therapy?

A.   The general answer is no. But there is little evidence on what may happen if you do, and research to find an answer is unlikely to ever take place. Some women with overwhelming symptoms who find no relief from alternative options, simply say they will take the risk in order to enhance their current quality of life.

Q.   I take continuous estrogen and cycled progestin and get a **period**. Is this always going to happen?

A.   This depends on whether you remain on the same medication. It is possible that you are taking a higher dose than is necessary, and a low dose regimen may stop the bleeding. Another alternate is to start a low dose combined estrogen and progestin combination.

Q.   Can I avoid the risk of bone fractures if I only use **calcium and vitamin D**?

A.   If you have normal bone density, exercise, and eat healthy you may not ever need anything. But if you are already at risk for fracture, an active drug is necessary.

Q.   My clinician wants to control my dose of hormones with regular **saliva tests**. Is this really necessary?

A.   Grab your wallet and your credit card and run away as fast as possible. Find a reputable clinician. We treat *symptoms* with the lowest effective dose of whatever drug we are using. *We do not treat saliva or blood levels.*

Q.   Are there any **questions** I really must ask my clinician at my first or subsequent visit?

A.   Absolutely yes. See page 178-180.

Q.   I have **irregular spotting** on my hormones and this has been going on for quite a while. Should I just ignore it?

Q.   Most definitely not. See your clinician She may need to do an endometrial biopsy, an in-office procedure in which a tiny instrument is passed through the cervix and a sample of the lining is taken and sent to the pathologist. Sometimes an ultrasound test will also be done.

Q.   What is the difference between **synthetic hormones and natural hormones**?

A.   A great question that confuses everybody. Natural hormones would be those made by the body. Synthetics are made in the laboratory. However, it is possible to make synthetics that are identical to the natural hormones. If the product is called estradiol, progesterone, or testosterone, it can be accepted as natural, whatever its source.

Q.   I have **varicose veins**. Does that preclude me from taking hormones?

A.   Varicose veins are not a rigid contraindication for hormones, but may carry an increased risk for blood clots in the legs. Accordingly, they should be carefully considered as a factor by your clinician.

Q.   Would **vaginal estrogen** affect my **male partner**?

A.   The usual dose is so low, any effect on the male is highly unlikely, and there are no descriptions in the scientific literature reporting any harm.

Q.   I am **lactose intolerant**, so how do I get enough **calcium in my diet**?

A.   There is good calcium in the bones of canned sardines and salmon. Spinach leaves are a reasonable source. The best would be to take a calcium supplement tablet, including vitamin D.

APPENDIX D

AUTHOR'S BIOGRAPHICAL SKETCH

Wulf H. Utian, MD, PhD, DSc.

Professor Emeritus of Reproductive Biology and Obstetrics and Gynecology, Case Western Reserve University School of Medicine (CWRU)

Consultant in Women's Health, The Cleveland Clinic Foundation

Scientific Director, Rapid Medical Research, Inc.

Executive Director Emeritus and Founding President, NAMS

Honorary Past President and Co-Founder, The International Menopause Society

Wulf Utian has the most unique personal history relating to the subject of menopause. As a young academic physician-researcher in 1967 he founded the Groote Schuur Menopause Research Clinic in Cape Town, South Africa, the world's first menopause research center. He completed a research PhD on the subject in 1970 at the University of Cape Town.

In the 1970's, working with two internationally renowned physician friends, now unfortunately both deceased, Pieter van Keep (Director General of the International Health Foundation in Geneva, Switzerland) and Robert Greenblatt (Director of Endocrinology at the Medical College of Georgia, in Augusta, Georgia, USA), he partnered with them in founding the International Menopause Society. Later he and Pieter van Keep launched the world's first scientific medical journal devoted to the Menopause, called Maturitas.

In 1989 Wulf Utian founded The North American Menopause Society (NAMS), and in 1994, with another friend, Isaac Schiff (OB/GYN Professor at Harvard and head of the department at the Massachusetts General Hospital in Boston), launched what is now the top scientific journal in the field, MENOPAUSE.

In 2007 he earned the Doctor Of Science (DSc) degree from the University of Cape Town, only the 11th time this degree has been awarded by the University in nearly 100 years. It is only given to those who have made a seminal difference in the advancement of some aspect

201

of medical science. His compilation of over 200 of his scientific publications in relation to all aspects of menopause fulfilled that rule.

Board Certified in Obstetrics and Gynecology and Reproductive Endocrinology, he is a Fellow of the Royal College of Obstetricians and Gynaecologists, the American College of Obstetricians and Gynecologists and the International College of Surgeons. He was Director of the Department of Obstetrics and Gynecology, University Hospitals of Cleveland and Chairman of the Department of Reproductive Biology, CWRU (1989-1999).

Dr. Utian is a specialist in the fields of gynecological endocrinology and infertility. He has been an innovator in several aspects of advanced reproductive technology. He has studied the metabolic and psychosocial aspects of estrogen and menopause for over 40 years. He is the recipient of numerous awards and research grants.

A strong advocate for women's health, Dr. Utian has achieved international recognition for his work and is interviewed regularly by the international media. He was honored by *Good Housekeeping* magazine in 1997 as "one of America's best physicians in women's health," by *Ladies Home Journal* in 1999 as one of the "top ten researchers in women's health," was the first recipient of the NAMS Lifetime Achievement Award in 1999, was honored by the Royal College of Obstetricians and Gynaecologists in 2000 for his achievements in the area of menopause, and in 2005 was awarded the Food and Drug Administration's Commissioner's Special Citation "for the collective outstanding performance of the 'Menopause and Hormones Information Campaign' that resulted in the launch of a national public awareness outreach campaign". In 2007 he became the first man to be honored by Speaking of Women's Health, a national women's education and advocacy program administered by the prestigious Cleveland Clinic, and in 2011 was admitted to the Speaking of Women's Health Hall of Fame.

His first non-medical book (THE UTIAN STRATEGY – is this my problem or is this your problem?) describing his problem solving strategy learned through his own life experiences was published in 2010.

Complete resume and communication information: www.UtianLLC.com

GLOSSARY

absorptiometry - *see* bone densitometry, DEXA

acute – sudden onset; opposite of chronic

administer – to give a treatment e.g. injection

adolescence – *see* puberty

AIDS – autoimmune deficiency disease caused by the HIV virus

alleviate – reduce, make less, improve or cure

amenorrhea – absence or loss of periods

anatomy – description of body structure and parts

androgens – steroid hormones with male-like effects

andropause – term used to refer to changes in men traversing middle age

anemia - reduced amount of red blood cells in circulation

antidepressants – drugs against depression; mood-elevating drugs. *See* SSRI

alternative medicine – see CAM

anticonvulsants – drugs that prevent seizures (fits)

anus – opening of lower bowel to outside

anxiety - feeling of concern or worry

artery – those blood vessels leaving the heart and going to the rest of the body

arthritis – inflammation of joint/s

atheromatosis - fatty disease of blood vessels characterized by plaque-like swellings on the inner arterial lining

atherosclerosis – hardening of the arteries

atrophic vaginitis – thinning and inflammation of vagina

atrophy – reduction in size, shriveling, shrinking

Ayurveda - meaning the science of life, is the traditional medicine of India

Bartholin's gland – two glands situated each side of vaginal entrance that secrete lubricating mucous with sexual arousal

biofeedback – a technique of using the mind to control or modify involuntary body functions

bioidentical hormones – an artificial term to describe natural hormones. *See* natural hormones

birth control pill – *see* oral contraceptive, OC

bisphosphonates – drugs used against osteoporosis to slow bone loss

bladder – the storage sac for collecting urine from the kidneys

blood clot - a lump congealed blood inside a blood vessel

blood stream – refers to flow of blood inside blood vessels

blood vessels – the tubes carrying blood, *see* arteries and veins

bone densitometry – an x-ray test measuring amount (density) of bone. *See* DEXA

brain – the large grey ball of nervous tissue inside the skull

breakthrough bleeding – vaginal bleeding occurring while taking oral contraceptives or hormone therapy

breakthrough ovulation - an unexpected fertility cycle with potential for pregnancy occurring after several months of missed periods

breast – milk-producing gland

calcium – a chemical substance, hardens bones and teeth

calories – a unit/quantity of energy in foods

CAM – complementary and alternative medicine, a group of diverse medical and health care systems, practices, and products that are not generally considered part of conventional medicine

cancer – abnormal tissue that infiltrates and destroys local tissue or breaks and spreads elsewhere

carcinoma - *see* cancer

castration – surgical removal of ovaries or testes

CE – see conjugated estrogen

CEE – see conjugated equine estrogen

cell – the basic unit or building block out of which the body is constructed

cervix – entrance of uterus, mouth of womb

change of life - term referring to few years before and after menopause. Transition from reproductive to postreproductive phase of life; also called climacteric.

cholesterol - an essential steroid in pathway to hormone production. Part of fatty substances in circulation that can be implicated with atheromatosis

chronic – present or progressing over a long period of time; opposite of acute

climacteric – *see* change of life

climacteric syndrome – combination of symptoms associated with climacteric

clitoris – the small structure on the vulva above the vaginal opening that responds to sexual stimulation

complaint - symptom that is bothersome enough to report to the clinician

complication – a bad outcome of a disease; and adverse effect of a medication

compounding – the process of mixing medications for individual prescriptions, usually in forms not available commercially

compounding pharmacy - drug store that fills prescriptions for compounded medications

compression fracture – crush breakage of a vertebra weakened by bone loss

computerized axial tomography (CAT scan) – technique of multiple x-ray images for diagnosis of disease

condom – latex or synthetic shield over penis to avoid pregnancy or sexually transmitted disease

congenital - abnormality at birth but not inherited

conjugated estrogen – a form of estrogen. *See* CE

conjugated equine estrogen – a form of estrogen obtained from pregnant mare's urine. *See* CEE

contraceptive – mechanism for preventing pregnancy

contraindication – reason for avoiding a medication

conventional medicine – Western or allopathic medicine as practiced by MD's

Cooper's ligament – fibrous bands anchoring breasts to chest wall

coronary artery disease - *see* atheromatosis. Can lead to blocking of arteries

coronary heart disease – atheromatosis of arteries that feed the heart (coronary arteries). *See* atheromatosis, atherosclerosis, CHD

corpus luteum – the yellow estrogen and progesterone producing body in the ovary that develops from the Graafian follicle

cortisone/cortisol/corticosteroids – steroid hormones produced by adrenal gland

culture – social behavior, customary beliefs including racial, religious, or social, normally passed from one generation to the next

cycle – a recurring series of events; to move in a circle

cyclic regimen/cyclical – medication taken on a regular basis with breaks or interruptions

cytotoxic agent - drugs poisonous to certain cells, used as cancer therapy

D & C – dilatation and curettage; surgical procedure in which cervix is stretched to allow an instrument into the uterus to scrape the inner surface

deficiency disease - disease resulting from lack of an essential substance for the body

degenerative arthritis – see osteoarthritis

DHEA – a male hormone precursor that can also convert to estrogen

diabetes – disease characterized by lack of control of sugars caused by insufficient insulin

diet-style – habit of healthy eating as opposed to diet

diuretic – medication for reducing water in the body

dosage – the exact or actual amount of a medication

drug – the term in medical practice to refer to a medication

dysfunction – an abnormal function

dysmenorrhea – cramps and pain with periods

dyspareunia - vaginal burning or any pain related to sexual intercourse

dysphoria – blue moods but not depression

edema – body swelling associated with abnormal excess of accumulated fluid

embryo – early structure resulting from fertilization of egg and sperm

endocrine gland – a body gland releasing its chemicals directly into the blood stream

endocrinologist – physician specializing in diseases of the endocrine glands and hormones

endometrial biopsy – procedure for sampling uterine lining

endometriosis - disease with islands of endometrial tissue in other parts of the body, usually in pelvis

endometrium – the lining of the uterine cavity

enterocele – a hernia of the bowel into the vaginal wall

environment - all external conditions, circumstances

equol – an active form of isoflavinoid/soy estrogen used for treatment of VMS

ERA/ERB – specific receptors called alpha or beta that attach to estrogen

ERT – estrogen replacement therapy

estrogen - female sex hormone, mostly produced by ovaries

estrogen receptor – sites in a cell that can attach to hormones and initiate the function of that cell

exocrine glands – glands that secret their products to the outside

FDA – the Food and Drug Administration

fertile – ability to have a baby

fertilization - successful combining of egg and sperm to form an embryo

fetus – the baby growing inside the uterus before birth

fibroid (fibromyoma) – a fibrous and muscle benign swelling in the wall of the uterus

flashes, hot – *see* hot flashes

fluid retention – *see* edema

follicle – *see* Graafian follicle

fracture – breakage of a bone

FRAX – a method of measuring level of risk of fracturing a bone

FSH – follicle simulating hormone; pituitary hormone directing Graafian follicle to grow

genital atrophy - reduction in size or wasting away of female sexual structures

genitals – female and male sex organs

gland – chemical producing body structure

gonad – sperm-producing testicle in the male and egg-producing ovary in the female

gonadotropin – hormone produced in the pituitary that stimulates function of the gonad

Graafian follicle – egg containing cellular sac in the ovary that produces estrogen

GnRH – hormone made in hypothalamus that stimulates pituitary to release gonadotropins

gynecologist – physician specializing in health care of women

holistic medicine - term used to indicate concern for the whole person, including not only the physical, but also the emotional, mental, and spiritual aspects

homeopathic medicine - unconventional Western system offers minute doses of specially prepared plant extracts to cure an illness

hormone – a chemical messenger produced by an endocrine gland

hot flashes - an intense sensation of heat spreading over arms, chest and face, followed by sweating and shivering, also called vasomotor symptoms (VMS)

hot flushes – *see* hot flashes

hypertension – high blood pressure

HRT – hormone replacement therapy, implies combination of estrogen and progestogen treatment

HT – hormone therapy, a term preferred to the old term HRT

Hypnotics - drugs to induce sleep or relaxation

hypothalamus – funnel shaped structure near base of brain that functions as a coordinating center

HSDD – human sexual desire disorder

hysterectomy – removal of uterus by surgery

idiosyncratic – an unusual or peculiar reaction to a drug by an individual

implant - hormone-containing pellet implanted under the skin

insomnia – problem with sleeping

isoflavones – see phytoestrogens

integrative medicine - practice that combines both conventional and CAM treatments for which there is evidence of safety and effectiveness

intrauterine device (IUD) – plastic device placed in uterus for contraception. After menopause can contain progestogen to safeguard the endometrium

jaundice – excess bile, usually result of liver disease, causing yellow body coloration

labia majora – the outer lips at the vaginal entrance

labia minora – the inner lips at the entrance to the vagina

laparoscope – a long, thin telescopic instrument used for viewing inside the abdominal cavity

laparotomy – surgical opening of the abdominal wall to explore inside

LH – luteinizing hormone, the pituitary hormone stimulating the release of the egg from the Graafian follicle and conversion into the corpus luteum

libido – sexual desire and drive

lipoprotein – a complex structure of fat and protein, multiple types in circulation

luteinizing hormone - -*see* LH

menarche – the first menstrual period

menopause – the final menstrual period

menstrual flow – the monthly period, blood coming out of vagina

menstrual irregularity – vaginal bleeding at irregular or unexpected times

menstrual period – *see* menstrual flow, indicates no pregnancy in that cycle

menstruation – the monthly period

mortality rate – number of deaths occurring per a certain number of the population

NAMS – the North American Menopause Society

natural estrogens – estrogens similar to those normally made by the body. *See* bioidentical hormones

nausea – the sensation of a need to vomit

NCCAM – National Center for Complementary and Alternative Medicine at NIH

NCMP – NAMS Certified Menopause Practitioner, certification achieved by examination

NIH – the National Institutes of Health

Nocturia – the urge to empty the bladder during the night

obese – extremely fat, overweight

observational study – a retrospective analysis of treated and untreated individuals in a community or selected population (e.g. nurses)

occlusion – a blockage, usually refers to a blood vessel
oophorectomy – surgical removal of one or both ovaries
orgasm – the sexual climax
ORWH – Office of Research on Women's Health
Osteoarthritis – use and usually age related inflammation of joints
osteoporosis – thinning of bone with susceptibility to fracture
ovariectomy – see oophorectomy
ovary – the female organ containing follicles with eggs and ability to produce hormone
ovulation – the release of the egg from the follicle in the ovary
paced respiration – a form of slow controlled breathing to reduce the severity or impact of hot flashes
PAP smear – cervical cancer test with scraping of cells from cervix
Parathyroid hormone PTH – a hormone that affects bone metabolism and is used to treat osteoporosis
pathology - the science of the study of disease in organs
pedometer – a small instrument to measure the number of steps taken when walking
pelvis – the bony basin around the lower body organs
perimenopause – the few years before and 12 months after the final menstrual period (menopause); time around menopause
period – see menstrual flow
pessary – plastic ring for supporting pelvic structures or delivering medications
pharmacology – science of the study of drugs
physiology – science of the study of the functions of the body
phytoestrogens - plant-derived compounds with estrogen-like biologic activity
pituitary gland – the small pea-like endocrine gland at the base of the brain
postmenopausal – refers to years after menopause
postmenopausal syndrome - cluster of symptoms that may be associated with menopause
prebiotics—non-digestible food ingredients that selectively stimulate the growth and/or activity of microorganisms already present in the body
primordial follicle – the early follicle in the ovary comprised of the egg surrounded by hormone-producing cells
probiotics—live microorganisms (usually bacteria) that are similar to microorganisms normally found in the human digestive tract and that may have beneficial effects
progesterone – the natural female hormone produced by the corpus luteum

progestin – a synthetic hormone with a progesterone-like effect

progestogen – collective term refers to progesterone and progestins

prolactin – a pituitary hormone that works on the breast

prolapse - dropping or sagging of uterus, bladder, and vagina due to loss of pelvic supports

psychology – science of the study of behavior

puberty - transition from childhood through onset of reproductive age

pubic hair – hair on the external genitalia

randomized controlled trial (RCT) - prospective research study comparing an active treatment against an inactive control with investigators' blinded to allocation

rank ligand inhibitor – a new generation of drugs to save and build bone

ratio – numerical comparison between one thing and another, for example risk and benefit (risk:benefit)

receptor – see estrogen receptor and ERA/ERB

regime – a plan for a course of treatment

renal failure – kidney failure

reproductive organs – ovaries, fallopian tubes, uterus, and vagina

risk:benefit ratio – *see* ratio

secrete - production and release of a substance from a gland

sexual intercourse – the act of making love

side effect – an undesirable effect produced by a drug

social – relates to the way a community is structured and thinks

somatic – relating to the body

speculum – the metal or plastic instrument that is inserted into the vagina to allow inspection of the interior, the cervix, and to take smears

spotting – irregular, slight bleeding between periods or on hormone treatments, but less than breakthrough bleeding

SSRI – see antidepressants

Statins – drugs to reduce blood levels of fats like cholesterol

stress incontinence – leaking of urine with coughing, sneezing, or other exertion

subcutaneous – under the skin

surgical menopause – menopause that results from bilateral oophorectomy

SWHR – Society for Women's Health Research

symptom - a feeling or sensation that alerts the body to something wrong

syndrome – a cluster set of symptoms put together as a group, e.g. menopause syndrome

synthetic hormones – hormones that are chemically created, but can be identical to natural hormones

testes – the male gonads that produces male hormone and sperm

testosterone - the male steroid hormone

therapy – treatment

thromboembolism – the breaking off of a blood clot, usually in leg or pelvis, that travels elsewhere via bloodstream, usually to lung

Tibolone – a steroidal drug with estrogenic, progestogenic and androgenic effects

traditional Chinese medicine TCM - includes acupuncture, herbal medicines, oriental massage, and other ancient techniques

tranquilizers – medications to reduce anxiety

transdermal – through the skin

urethra – the pipe from the bladder to the outside carrying urine

uterine prolapse – *see* prolapse

uterus – the womb

vagina – the muscular tube for sex; also is the birth canal

vaginal ring – *see* pessary

vaginal smear – scraping of cells from the vaginal wall for laboratory testing

varicose veins – dilated veins, especially in legs, with incompetent internal valves

vein – the blood vessels carrying blood from the body back to the heart

vulva – the outside parts of the female genitalia

womb – the uterus

xerosis – dry skin

INDEX

HOW TO ORDER

CHANGE *YOUR* MENOPAUSE is available as a paperback print edition or an eBook at all popular online booksellers.

To order the print edition of this book or the eBook, go to any major online bookseller (Amazon.com, BN.Com, Kalahari.net etc.) and enter the book title, or the author's name, Wulf Utian, in the search box. Click on the book's title when the page comes up to access details and ordering information.

If you found CHANGE *YOUR* MENOPAUSE to be of value, please post a review for it on Amazon.com.

BULK ORDERS: For bulk order discounts contact the author directly at <u>wulf@utianllc.com</u>

SHARE AN EXPERIENCE OF YOUR OWN

We all have unique experiences that have lessons to teach or to learn. **If you have an interesting story to share, please email me at:** <u>wulf@utianllc.com</u>

You can also **blog a comment** through my website on one of the subjects under the heading WHAT'S UP at: <u>www.UtianLLC.com</u>

We Survived
THE
HOLOCAUST

Also by Elaine Landau

ALZHEIMER'S DISEASE

BLACK MARKET ADOPTION AND
THE SALE OF CHILDREN

COWBOYS

INTERESTING INVERTEBRATES: A LOOK AT SOME
ANIMALS WITHOUT BACKBONES

JUPITER

LYME DISEASE

MARS

NAZI WAR CRIMINALS

NEPTUNE

ROBERT FULTON

SATURN

THE SIOUX

SURROGATE MOTHERS

TROPICAL RAIN FORESTS
AROUND THE WORLD

WE HAVE AIDS

WILDFLOWERS AROUND THE WORLD